Hodder Cambridge Primary
Science

Learner's Book

Stage 3

Hellen Ward

Series editors: Rosemary Feasey and Deborah Herridge

Acknowledgements

The Publisher is extremely grateful to the following schools for their comments and feedback during the development of this series:

Avalon Heights World Private School, Ajman
The Oxford School, Dubai
Al Amana Private School, Sharjah
British International School, Ajman
Wesgreen International School, Sharjah
As Seeb International School, Al Khoud

The publisher would like to thank the following for permission to reproduce copyright material.

p.64 https://www.cdc.gov/features/handwashing/; **p.71** www.a2magic.com Jeff Wawrzaszek; **p.72** http://www.optical-illusionist.com/illusions/young-lady-or-old-woman-illusion

Photo credits

p.6 © Elena Elisseeva/123rf; **p.7** © Sally and Richard Greenhill/Alamy Stock Photo; **p.11** *t* © Kathleen V Salisbury; **p.11** *b* © Korkeng/Shutterstock; **p.13** *tl*, **p.54**, **p.55** (all), **p.68** (all), **p.69**, **p.76**, **p.92**, **p.100** *b*, **p.101** *t*, **p.104** *t* (all), **p.125**, **p.141** © Hachette UK; **p.13** *tr* © C Squared Studios/Photodisc/Getty Images/Just Flowers 2; **p.14** *t* © Derek Harris/Alamy Stock Photo; **p.14** *b* © Lucky-photographer/Shutterstock; **p.15** © Hellen Ward; **p.16** *tl* © C Squared Studios/Photodisc/Getty Images/Just Flowers 2; **p.16** *tc* © Stockbyte/Getty Images/Flowers SD119; **p.16** *c* © Stockbyte/Getty Images Ltd/Health SD124; **p.16** *tr* © Jiang Hongyan/ Shutterstock; **p.17** © Borzywoj/Fotolia; p.18 © Ivan Kmit/Fotolia; **p.20** *tl* © Dmitry Naumov/Fotolia; **p.20** *tr*, **p.140** © Formiktopus/Fotolia; **p.22** © Mironmax Studio/Shutterstock; **p.26** © Emjay Smith/Shutterstock; **p.31** © Flaudgirl/Fotolia; **p.32** © FAUP/Fotolia; **p.33** *t* © Iryna Art/Shutterstock; **p.33** *b* © Zuma Press, Inc./Alamy Stock Photo; **p.34** © Anna Kucherova/Shutterstock; **p.39** *bl* © Lindsay Franklin/Shutterstock; **p.39** *br* © Eric Isselee/Shutterstock; **p.46** *t* © Inesbazdar/123rf; **p.46** *c* © Alistair Berg/Getty Images; **p.47** © Cathy Yeulet/123rf; **p.50** © Brian Jackson/Fotolia; **p.51** © Stockbyte/Getty Images/Entertainment & Leisure CD35; **p.52** © Sally Wallis/Shutterstock; **p.57** *t* © Apollofoto/Shutterstock; **p.57** *c* © Images of Africa Photobank/Alamy Stock Photo; **p.58** © Hieng Ling Tie/123rf; **p.59** © Avava/Shutterstock; **p.63** © Robert Kneschke/Shutterstock; **p.64** © TinnaPong/Shutterstock; **p.66** © Hongqi Zhang/123rf; **p.67**, **p.85** © Riccardo Mayer/Shutterstock; **p.75** © OlgaLis/Fotolia; **p.77**, **p.144** © Deyan Georgiev/123rf; **p.81** © Nancy R. Cohen/Photodisc/Getty Images/Eat, Drink, Dine 48; **p.82** © Dr David Furness, Keele University/Science Photo Library; p.84 *t* © Aerogondo/Fotolia; **p.84** *b* © Historical/Contributor/Getty Images; **p.86** © Imagestate Media (John Foxx)/Vol 18 Golddisc I; **p.90** © Boaz Rottem/Alamy Stock Photo; **p.96** *t* © Snake3d/123rf; **p.96** *c* © Kornwalai Bunkijrungpaisarn/123rf; **p.96** *b* © PNAS: Proceedings of the National Academy of Sciences of the United States of America; **p.98** © Tetra Images/Alamy Stock Photo; **p.99** © Kayo/Alamy Stock Photo; **p.100** *t* © Iurii Levonchuk/123rf; **p.101** *b* © Disruptive Materials AB; **p.102** © Eugene Sergeev/123rf; **p.103** © Knumina Studios/Shutterstock; **p.104** *b*, **p.113** *c* © Adrian Niwa/123rf; **p.105** *tl* © andristkacenko/123rf; **p.105** *tr* © Grigvovan/123rf; **p.105** *bl* © Suljo/123rf; **p.105** *br* © Picsfive/123rf; **p.106** © Karl Kost/Alamy Stock Photo; **p.108**, **p.113** *cr* © Imagestate Media (John Foxx)/Minimal Colour Concepts SS117; **p.110** *t* Richard Williams/Potatopak Ltd; **p.110** *cr* © Sergio Stakhnyk/Shutterstock; **p.110** *b* © Hugh Threlfall/Alamy Stock Photo; **p.111** *t* , **p.113** *cl* © Hugh Threlfall/Alamy Stock Photo; **p.111** *b* , **p.113** *t* © Christiaan Maats; **p.117** *c* © Duncan Noakes/Fotolia; **p.117** *cr* © Steven Pepple/Fotolia; **p.119, p.121** (all) © TickiT® Educational Products; **p.128** *t* © Izlan Somai/Shutterstock; **p.128** *c* © Rtimages/Shutterstock; **p.128** *b* © Lovethephoto/Alamy Stock Photo; **p.132** © CnOPhoto/Shutterstock; **p.134** © Bikerider London/Shutterstock.

t = top, *b* = bottom, *l* = left, *r* = right, *c* = centre

Practice text exam-style questions and sample answers have been written by the author(s).

Note: While every effort has been made to check the instructions for practical work described in this book carefully, schools should conduct their own risk assessments in accordance with local health and safety requirements.

Every effort has been made to trace all copyright holders, but if any have been inadvertently overlooked the Publishers will be pleased to make the necessary arrangements at the first opportunity.

Although every effort has been made to ensure that website addresses are correct at time of going to press, Hodder Education cannot be held responsible for the content of any website mentioned in this book. It is sometimes possible to find a relocated web page by typing in the address of the home page for a website in the URL window of your browser.

Hachette UK's policy is to use papers that are natural, renewable and recyclable products and made from wood grown in sustainable forests. The logging and manufacturing processes are expected to conform to the environmental regulations of the country of origin.

Orders: please contact Bookpoint Ltd, 130 Milton Park, Abingdon, Oxon OX14 4SB. Telephone: (44) 01235 827720. Fax: (44) 01235 400454. Lines are open from 9.00–5.00, Monday to Saturday, with a 24 hour message answering service. You can also order through our website www.hoddereducation.com

© Hellen Ward 2017

Published by Hodder Education

An Hachette UK Company

Carmelite House, 50 Victoria Embankment, London EC4Y 0DZ

Impression number   5 4 3 2 1

Year   2019 2018 2017

All rights reserved. Apart from any use permitted under UK copyright law, no part of this publication may be reproduced or transmitted in any form or by any means, electronic or mechanical, including photocopying and recording, or held within any information storage and retrieval system, without permission in writing from the publisher or under licence from the Copyright Licensing Agency Limited. Further details of such licences (for reprographic reproduction) may be obtained from the Copyright Licensing Agency Limited, Saffron House, 6–10 Kirby Street, London EC1N 8TS.

Cover illustration © Steve Evans

Illustrations by Vian Oelofsen, Jeanne du Plessis, Alex van Houwelingen

Typeset in FS Albert 15 on 17pt by IO Publishing CC

Printed in Slovenia

A catalogue record for this title is available from the British Library

9781471883996

Contents

Being a scientist

| What does a scientist do? | 4 |
| How to do a fair test | 5 |

Biology

Unit 1 Plants	6
Unit 2 Life processes	28
Unit 3 Unit 3 Keeping healthy	46
Unit 4 The senses	66
Practice test 1: Biology	86

Chemistry

| Unit 5 Material properties | 90 |
| Practice test 2: Chemistry | 114 |

Physics

| Unit 6 Forces and motion | 116 |
| Practice test 3: Physics | 138 |

Glossary

| Scientific dictionary | 140 |

Being a scientist

What does a scientist do?

Scientists are people who are interested in the world around them. They ask questions. Then they find answers by testing their ideas in different ways.

Scientists look for similarities and differences. They sort things into groups so that they can identify, name and classify them (such as flowers in a field).

Scientists compare what happens. For example, they put objects into water to find out if they float or sink.

Scientists test their ideas. They observe what effect one thing has on another thing in an investigation. They try to keep things fair.

Scientists share what they find out about the world. They read books, search the internet and watch videos to find new information.

Shoe length	Number of people
21 cm	1
24 cm	3
25 cm	3
26 cm	2
27 cm	8
28 cm	5
29 cm	1
30 cm	1
31 cm	1

Scientists make observations using all their senses. They make notes and draw pictures to record what they find out. Scientists keep this information.

Scientific questions must be measurable. Scientists look for patterns in their results.

Being a scientist

How to do a fair test

Read steps 1 to 11. Find out what scientists think about and do to carry out a fair test. A fair test is one way to investigate a scientific question.

① Think about what you want to find out. You will need to ask a scientific question – a question that will let you investigate, test and measure the results.

② Think about what you will do to answer your question. Can you think of a way to test it?

③ What equipment will you need to help you? You might need measuring equipment such as a ruler.

④ When you carry out your fair test, you will need to decide what thing you will change and what effect you will measure. These are called variables (factors).

⑤ You might think of many things to change in your test. You must only change one variable (factor). Everything else must stay the same.

⑥ While doing your fair test, you will observe changes. You will need to measure the changes (such as time).

⑦ You need to record your observations (data) to remember what happened. You could use a table. Record what you changed in one column. Record what you measured in another column.

⑧ Sometimes you can put the data in your table into a chart. This will help you to see the pattern.

⑨ When you have finished your fair test, use what you have found out to answer your question. This is your conclusion.

⑩ Was your test a good test? Do you trust your results? How can you improve your test?

⑪ After carrying out a fair test, you may have more questions. To find the answers, you must carry out more investigations.

5

Unit 1 Plants

What do you know about plants?

Scientific words
flower
stem
leaf
roots
function

1

Draw a mind map of everything you know about plants.

a What parts do all plants have? Use these words.

> flower   stem   leaf   roots

b Do you know the **function** (purpose) of each part?

Can you name the different parts of a plant?

2

Write a letter to new learners at your school. Use a labelled picture (diagram) to explain the meaning of the word 'plant'. Try to use the words in the scientific words box.

Talk partners

Discuss your mind map with a partner. Pretend that learners who have never seen plants before are visiting your school. How will you explain what a plant is?

Plants

Looking closely at plants

You will need...
- hand lens
- clipboard
- paper
- pencil

Walk around your school grounds or a garden. What plants can you find?

a Choose a plant and draw it. Using the hand lens, look at the different parts of the plant. What do you notice?
Label each part you can see. Write anything interesting such as: *The leaves are red. They have bumps and lines running through them.*

b Are there any parts of the plant you cannot see? Draw your ideas of what you cannot see on the diagram.

c Write your ideas about the function of each part you have drawn, for example:
I think the leaves are for ....
I think the flowers are for ....

d Do you know the name of your plant?
If not, try to find out.

Talk partners

Compare your diagram with a partner's diagram. Which parts of the plant have you both drawn? Which parts of the plant are different? Discuss your ideas about the function of each part of the plants.

7

Unit 1 Plants

Living things

1

Look back at your diagram from Activity 1 on page 7.
How do you know that the plant is a **living** thing? What **evidence** (proof) is there? Write down your ideas. Think about what a plant needs to **grow** and how it behaves.

Scientific words
living
evidence
grow

2

Samir came home and saw what her baby brother had done to her plant! Do you think the plant is still living? She created this table to find out.

Evidence that the plant is living	Evidence that the plant is not alive
It has leaves, roots and a stem.	The leaves and the stem are not joined.
There is soil.	The plant can no longer stand alone.
It grew from a seed.	The roots look broken and damaged.
It has a flower.	The leaves are curled and dried up.

a Look at the table that Samir created. Which statements are true, but do not make the plant living?

b Which statements do you think are false?

c Create your own table. Include the information that you think is correct. Add some statements of your own. Decide if the plant is living or not alive.

Plants

Life cycle of a plant

Think like a scientist!

Plants grow from **seeds**. Seeds are living things. A seed can **germinate** (start growing), but it needs certain **conditions** (things) to make this happen. **Seedlings** are young plants. They grow into mature (older) plants. These plants **produce** flowers. After the flowers die, they make new seeds for the plant. When the seeds are planted the cycle begins again.

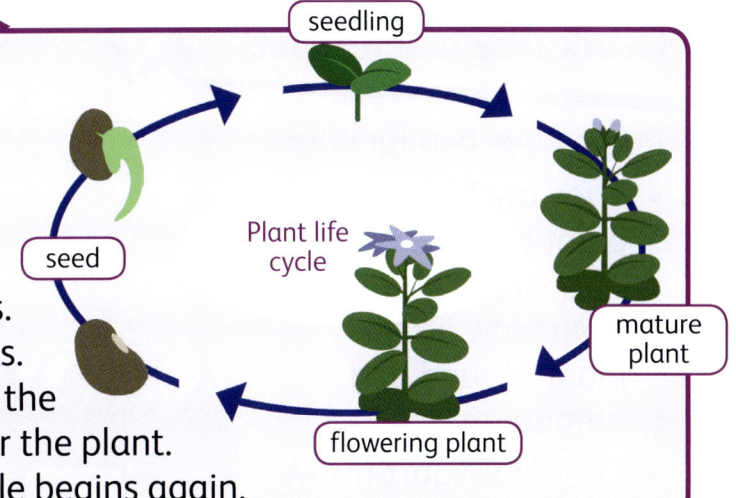

1

Find out if big seeds germinate before small seeds.
a Predict which seed will germinate first and why.
b Soak some kitchen towels in water.
  • Place a towel in each pot. Add a different-sized seed on top of each towel.
  • Place the pots in a warm (sunny) place. Water them every day.
c You need to carry out a fair test. Which things should stay the same?
d Record your results in a table like this:

You will need...
- small, medium and large seeds
- plant pots
- kitchen towels
- water

Size of seed	Prediction	After 3 days	After 5 days	After 7 days
small				
medium				
large				

e Which seed germinated first? Was your prediction correct? What are your conclusions? Does the size of a seed affect how long it takes to germinate?

What conditions do seeds need to grow?

Scientific words
seeds
germinate
conditions
seedlings
produce

9

Unit 1 Plants

 **Roots**

Scientific words
anchor
transport
nutrients

Think like a scientist!

Roots have two functions:
- They **anchor** (fix) the plant into the ground. This stops the wind from blowing the plant around and damaging it.
- They **transport** (move) water and **nutrients** (the plant needs these to grow) from the ground into the plant.

1

Observe and measure what happens to bean seeds as they grow. Create a growing wall.
- Soak one bean overnight in water.
- Place this bean in some wet cotton wool at the bottom of a clear plastic bag. Label the bag with the date and pin it onto your growing wall.
- Plant a new bean every day for two weeks. Repeat the two steps above each time.
- Make sure you keep the cotton wool wet in all the bags.

You will need...
- runner bean seeds
- water
- small plastic bags
- cotton wool
- pins
- ruler

a Record the changes you see in an 'Observation diary'. On which day did the roots start to grow? Do not forget to measure the roots each day! Use a ruler.

b How long were the roots of the first bean seed on day 10?

c Do the beans only have one root?

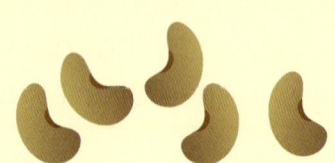

10

Plants

Measuring roots

1

Jasmine looked at the picture of switch grass and asked: 'Do the tallest plants have the longest roots?'
Help Jasmine to plan a way to find out.

a Write down your ideas. Think about:
- Where can she find plants to use?
- What equipment will she need?
- What will she need to measure?
- What types of plants may she pull out of the ground?
- Which plants should she not pull up?
- How can she record her results?

b Try Jasmine's investigation. What are your conclusions to her question? Use a table like this to help you.

switch grass

roots

Name of plant	Height of plant above ground	Length of roots below ground

Did you know?

The tree with the deepest roots is a wild fig tree at Echo Caves, near Ohrigstad, in the province of Mpumalanga, South Africa. Its roots go down 120 metres!

11

Unit 1 Plants

Comparing roots and heights

Think like a scientist!

Class 3 created a **bar chart** to compare root length and height of four plants. They measured each plant above ground. They recorded its height (blue bar). They also recorded its root length (red bar). They found that the little bluestem grass has roots that measure 2 m. Its height is 1 m. So the roots are 1 m longer than its height.

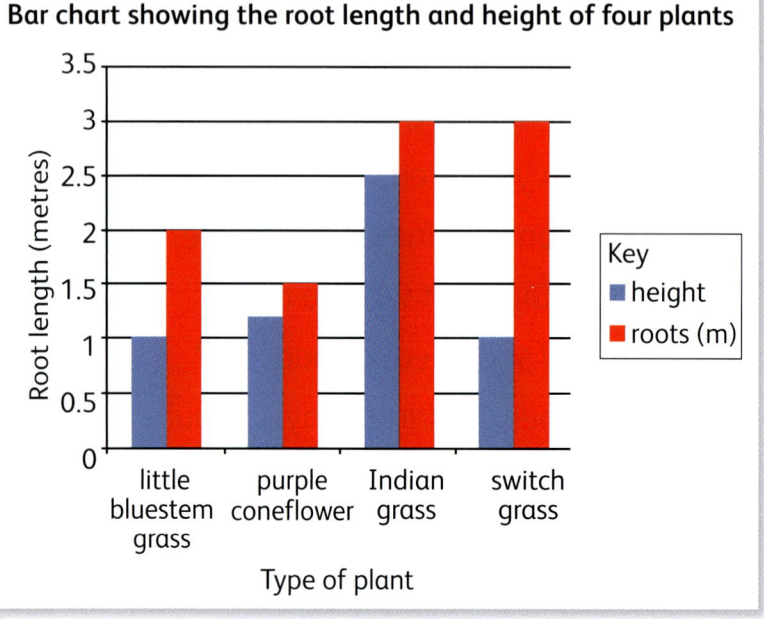

Bar chart showing the root length and height of four plants

1

Look at the bar chart.

Think of three questions that you could ask about this bar chart. Write each question on a sticky note.

- Make one question easy. Everyone in your class should be able to answer it.
- Make one question quite difficult – a little more challenging.
- Make one question very difficult. Only you may be able to answer it!

Scientific word
bar chart

Remember that you must know the answers yourself, and the information must be on the graph. Ask another pair of learners to answer your questions while you answer their questions.

12

Plants

Roots as an anchor

Think like a scientist!

roots

All plants have roots. The roots anchor (fix) the plant to the ground. This prevents it from breaking, bending, pulling, or falling over.

Look at the bean seeds you planted in Activity 1 on page 10. Are the roots anchored to anything?

Did you know?

Scientists found a spruce tree with 82,500 roots! Half of these roots were in the first 30 cm of the soil (the length of a ruler).

1

You will need...
- small pot plant
- hand lens

Carefully remove the plant from its pot. Gently tip the plant slightly so that it slides out.

a What do you observe about the roots of the plant?

b Look at the roots through a hand lens. What do you notice?

c Would the roots look the same if the plant was not growing in the pot?

d How are the roots anchoring the plant to stop it from falling over in the pot?

Be careful!

Take the plant out of the pot very gently. Do not break any part of it! Once you have finished observing the roots, slide the plant back into the pot carefully.

13

Unit 1 Plants

Stems

Think like a scientist!

The roots of a plant transport water and nutrients to the stem. Stems have two functions:
- They help to transport (move) water and nutrients to the leaves. Stems also transport food (made in the leaves) to other parts of the plant.
- They support the leaves and flowers.

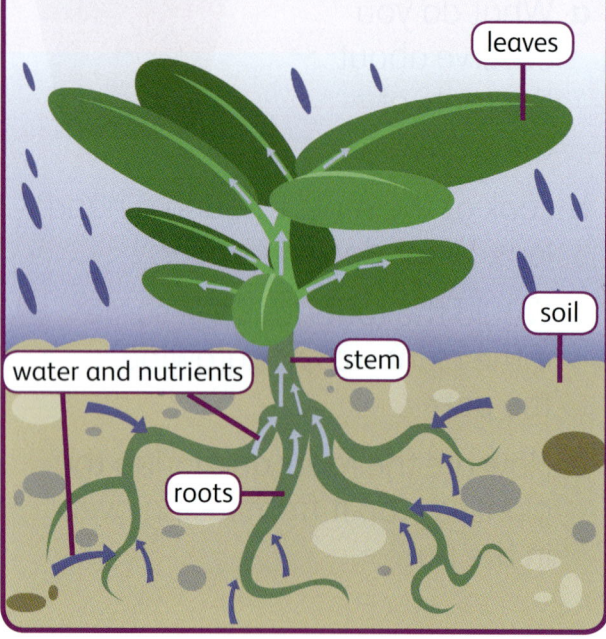

1

a Look at the stems of different plants in your school grounds or local area. If possible, take photographs to record what you find.

b Make notes about the stems. Write and draw how they are the same and how they are different.

c Share what you have found out about stems with a partner.

Did you know?

A tree that grows in California in the USA is called 'General Sherman'. It is not the tallest or widest tree in the world. Nor is it the oldest tree in the world. General Sherman holds the record for being the largest single stem tree on the Earth!

General Sherman tree

14

Plants

Tulip test

1

Senara and Iben placed some cut flowers in water. After a while, they noticed that the water level in the jar dropped. They asked each other: 'Where did the water go?' They decided to find out. They put some white tulips, the same length, in jars of different-coloured water. Look at the picture. The next day the flowers looked like this.

a Why do you think the flowers were different colours?

b What happened to the coloured water?

c How did the colour get into the flowers?

d Do you think each colour was transported equally?

e Why was it not a fair test?

Think about what must stay the same in this test to make it fair.
Hint: If they had left one flower in ordinary water, what colour would the tulip be?

Talk partners

Explain to a partner what you would do differently in Activity 1. Why?

Did you know?

Cut flowers usually have no roots. Water and nutrients are transported directly into the stem from the water in the jar or vase.

15

Unit 1 Plants

Stem investigation

1

Senara and Iben decided to find out what would happen to a white tulip when they split the stem in half. They cut the stem carefully with scissors. Then they placed a balloon filled with different-coloured food dye around the bottom of each half of the stem.

a What happened to the flower of the white tulip? Why?

b What do you think might happen if they cut the stem into thirds (three parts) and add another balloon of a different colour?

2

Senara and Iben wanted to know if the colour changes (in Activity 1 on page 15) happen in all plants. They selected four plants to test this.

tulip · carnation · celery · Chinese leaves

This table shows their results.

Type of plant stem	Time taken to change colour (hours)
tulip	5
carnation	4
celery	8
Chinese leaves	3

a Did all the plants transport water and dye? How do you know?

b Which plant was the quickest?

c Which plant was the slowest?

d What equipment would you need to be able to try the investigation in class?

e Create a bar chart from Senara and Iben's results.

Plants

 Types of leaves

Think like a scientist!

There are many types of leaves. Some are **simple leaves** because there is only one leaf. **Compound leaves** have **leaflets** (smaller leaves that form one leaf). Scientists describe the shape of leaves as **lobed, serrate** or **entire**.
Some leaves come from **evergreen** plants (those that have leaves all year). Some leaves come from **deciduous** plants (those that do not have have leaves all year).

1

You will need...
- magnifying glass
- different leaves from local plants

Collect different types of leaves from your local area.

a Sort the leaves into simple and compound leaves.

b Now sort your simple leaves according to its shape: lobed, serrate or entire.

Challenge yourself!

Sort your leaves from Activity 1 into 'evergreen' and 'deciduous'. You may need to do some research first. What similarities and differences do you notice about the two types of leaves?

Scientific words
simple leaves
compound leaves
leaflets
lobed
serrate
entire
evergreen
deciduous

leaves from an evergreen, deciduous tree

17

Unit 1 Plants

Looking at leaves

You will need...
- hand lens
- a leaf from a local plant

Choose a leaf. Use a hand lens to look at it carefully. Is the leaf identical (the same) on both sides?

a Draw and label both sides of your leaf. Add information to your diagram about the type of leaf it is, and its shape. Try to use some of the words in the scientific words box on page 17.

b Touch your leaf. What does it feel like? Does it have hairs? Is it waxy or is it spongy? Why do you think your leaf has these **features**?
Find out more about the plant that your leaf comes from. Add the information to your diagram.

c What size is your leaf? Does the size tell you anything about the plant that it comes from?

d Are the leaves symmetrical (the same on both sides) on the branch?

e Is your leaf from an evergreen or deciduous plant?

Did you know?

Plants can do amazing things. They can turn **sunlight**, water and **air** into food! The leaves are important because they collect sunlight for the plant. If the leaves do not get any sunlight they cannot make food. The leaves will not stay green and the plant will die.

Scientific words
features
sunlight
air

Plants

Leaf investigation

Think like a scientist!

The stem transports nutrients and water to the leaves. Plants use only a small amount of this water. If you use a hand lens to look at the back of a leaf, you will see **pores** (small dots). Scientists call these pores **stomata**. Plants are very clever – they open the stomata to let in gas (air) and let out water and gas that they do not need. Scientists call this process **transpiration**. Plants also transpire to keep cool.

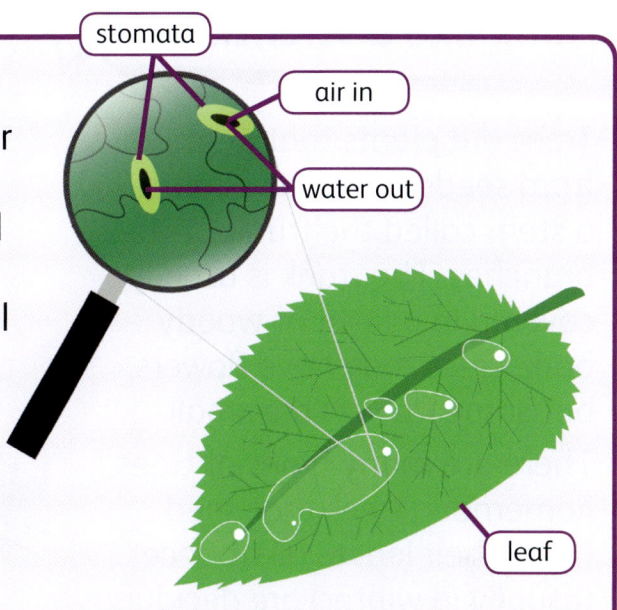

1

You will need...
- different types of leaves
- clear plastic sealable bags
- tray
- sunny windowsill

Try this test: Use two similar leaves. Place one in a sealed plastic bag on the tray. Place the other leaf on the tray without a plastic bag. Add a sealed empty bag to the tray.

a Predict and write what you think will happen to the leaves.

b Place the tray in sunshine on a windowsill.
Check the tray after two hours. Record any changes.

c What has happened to the leaves? Try to use some of the words in the scientific words box to explain your answer.

d Where do you think the liquid in the bag with the leaf came from?

e What could the liquid be?

f Why is it important to include an empty bag in your test?

Scientific words
pores
stomata
transpiration

19

Unit 1 Plants

Trees

Think like a scientist!

Trees are plants that germinate from seeds. Trees have roots, a stem called the trunk, and branches. The trunk is usually covered in a layer of woody bark. Trees may have flowers, but some flowers are small.

There are many types of trees. Remember, trees that shed (lose) their leaves all at once (usually in winter) are deciduous trees. Evergreen trees also shed leaves, but not all at the same time. They still have leaves during winter.

evergreen

deciduous

1

Sketch a tree that you can see in your school grounds or local area.

a Label the trunk, leaves, branches and roots.

b Does the tree have flowers?

c What does the bark feel like?

d Find out the name of the tree. Is it evergreen or deciduous?

Scientific words
survey
species

Challenge yourself!

Do a **survey** to find out about the trees in your area.
Take photographs to record the different trees. Collect a sample leaf if possible. Only take leaves that have fallen off the tree.

a Back in class, do some research to find out the names of the trees.

b Sort the leaves into ones from evergreen and deciduous trees.

c Which trees have simple leaves? Which have compound leaves?

d How many of each **species** (type) of tree are there? Present your results on a bar chart.

20

Plants

How trees grow

1

Inside a trunk, each ring represents (stands for) one year's growth.

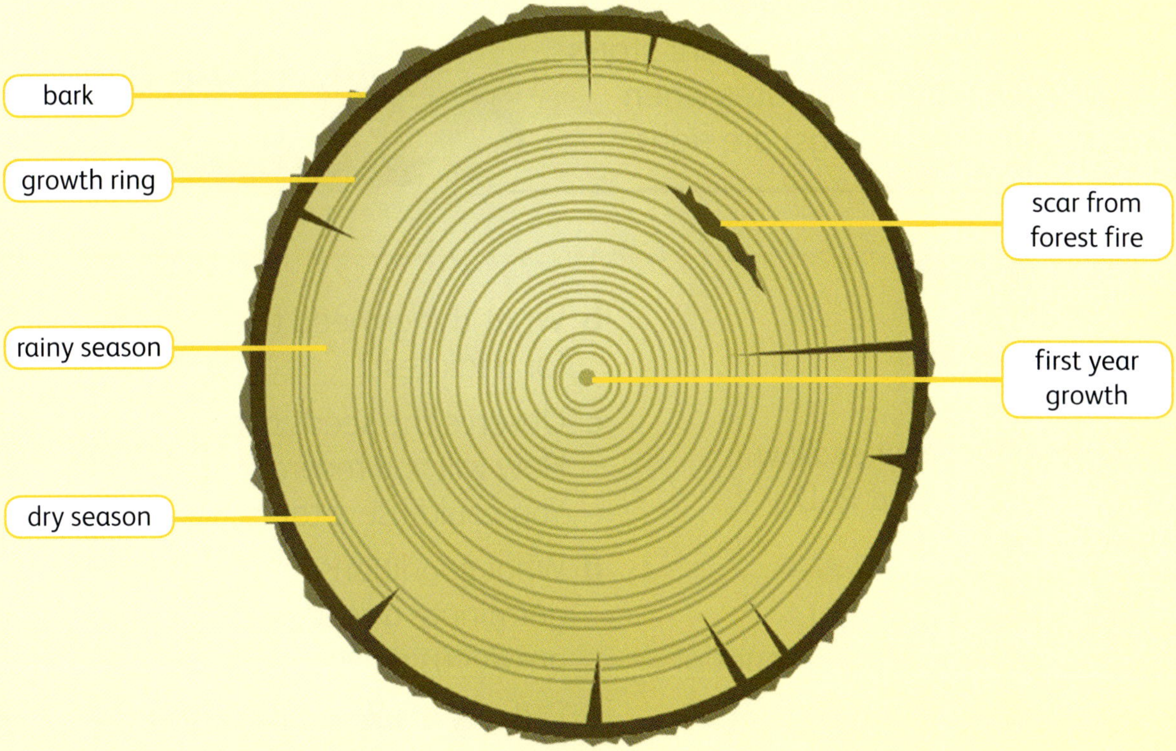

- bark
- growth ring
- rainy season
- dry season
- scar from forest fire
- first year growth

Some trees may grow for hundreds of years. You can find out how old some trees are by counting their rings. Each year the tree grows and a new ring is formed.

a Look at the picture. Try to work out how old the tree is.

b Are there any thin rings? What does this mean?

c Can you see any thicker rings? What does this mean?

Challenge yourself!

How do you think the weather affected the growth of the tree? Write an explanation.

21

Unit 1 Plants

 Conditions needed to germinate seeds

Think like a scientist!

After a flower dies, it produces (makes) seeds. Then the cycle of the plant starts again. A seed only germinates when certain conditions (things) are right.

sunflower seeds

1

You will need...
- 20 seeds
- four empty pots or shallow containers, marked A–D
- kitchen towels

Test the seeds in different conditions. Change the amount of water and warmth (sunlight) that the seeds receive. Do these things:

- Pot A – put five seeds on kitchen towel in a pot, no water and no warmth (sunlight).
- Pot B – put five seeds on kitchen towel in a pot with no water but with warmth (sunlight).
- Pot C – put five seeds on kitchen towel in a pot with water but with no warmth (sunlight).
- Pot D – put five seeds on kitchen towel in a pot with water and warmth (sunlight).

a Will all the seeds germinate? Make a prediction for each pot.

b What things need to stay the same for a fair test?

c Observe the seeds over one week. How will you record your results? You could use a table.

d What conditions are needed to germinate a seed? Explain your answer using your results.

e Did any results surprise you? Why?

Talk partners

What conditions do seeds need to germinate? Discuss your ideas with a partner. How could you check if you are right?

How long do you think it will take for the first seed to germinate?

22

Plants

Temperature and growth

Scientific word
temperature

1

Ayanna and her class wanted to find out if **temperature** affects the growth of plants. They placed two identical plants (A and B) in different temperatures. They measured the weight (in grams) that the plants gained after a few days in each temperature. Both plants weighed 0.5 g at the start of the test.

They knew that the more weight a plant gained, the more it had grown. They presented their results in this bar chart. Answer the questions.

Plant A was put in a place that was 5 °C.

Plant B was put in a place that was 20 °C.

Both plants were given the same amount of water and light.

a Use the results to write a sentence comparing what happened to plant A and plant B.

b How did Ayanna and her class make the test fair?

c Look at the results to write a conclusion: Does temperature effect the growth of plants? Use these words:

(results) (conclusion)

(because) (plant)

(temperature) (weight (grams))

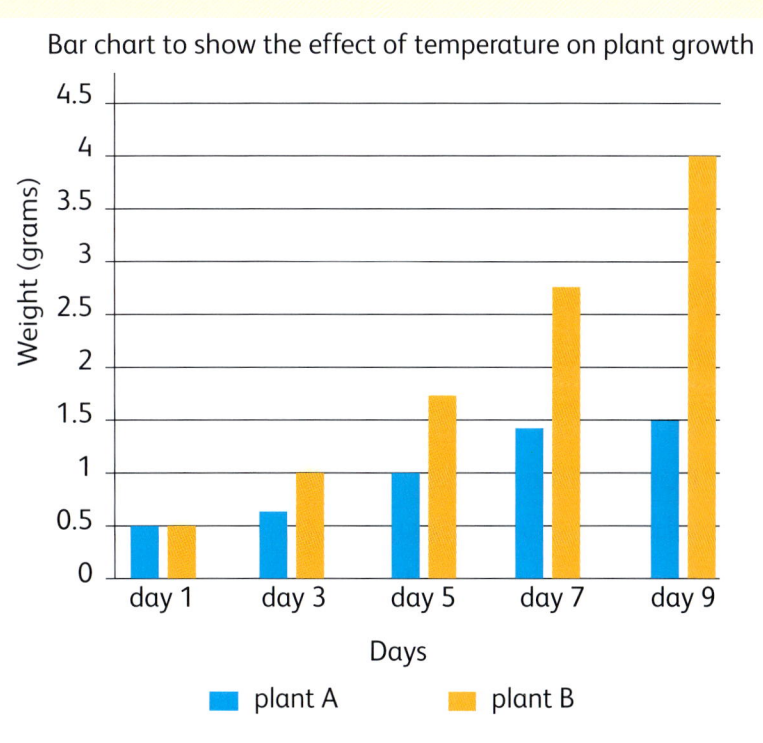

Bar chart to show the effect of temperature on plant growth

Unit 1 Plants

Try the temperature test

> **Talk partners**
>
> Discuss these questions with a partner:
> - Which type of plant would you use to test the **effect** of temperature?
> - Where would you put the plants?
> - How would you ensure that the test was fair?

1

a Plan a test to check the conclusions in Activity 1 on page 23. Use your discussion from the Talk partners activity above. Draw and label a diagram to show what you will do. Make sure you include:
- the equipment you will use
- the types of plants you will use
- where you will put the plants
- how you will make it a fair test
- what you will measure
- how you will record your result
- how many days you will need to do the test.

b Do your test and record your results.

c What are your conclusions and why?

d Present your results in a bar chart.

Scientific word
effect

Think about the things you will change and what needs to stay the same.

24

Plants

Changing conditions of a plant

Think like a scientist!

You know that seeds need water to germinate. You also know that plants grow best in sunlight and at a warm temperature. Now you will discover what happens when you change these **conditions**.

Scientific word
conditions
healthy

1

Rocco and Sara kept identical (the same) **healthy** plants in different conditions for one week to find out what would happen. This is what the plants looked like at the end of the week:

a Which plant do you think still looks healthy? Why?
b Which plant is now the least healthy? What evidence (clues) are you using?
c Place the plants in order from healthiest to least healthy.
d Match each condition in the boxes below to a plant in the pictures above. Why did you choose each condition?

| no warmth | no sunlight | sunlight, water and warmth | no water |

25

Unit 1 Plants

Plants we grow for food

Think like a scientist!

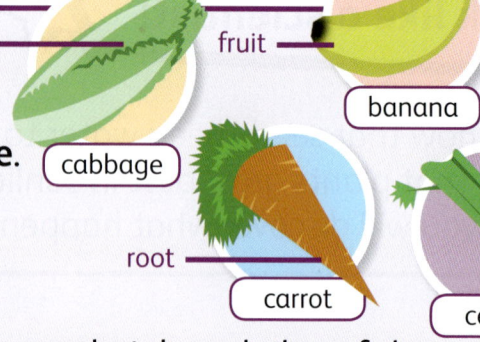

Humans and other animals often use plants as food. The plants we eat are **edible**. Edible plants include some plant leaves, stems and roots. Some plants produce (make) the **fruits** that we eat.

plants in a polytunnel

Farmers use their knowledge of the conditions that plants need to produce the food we eat. They make sure that plants get enough water, sunlight and the right temperatures. This way, farmers can grow large amounts of food at the same time. In some places, the temperature is not good for plants all year round. In this case, farmers grow plants in glasshouses (greenhouses) and polytunnels.

How does a glasshouse and a polytunnel help plants to grow?

Scientific words
edible
fruits

Talk partners

Talk to a partner about the plants you have eaten today.
Discuss and make a list of the different plants and their parts.

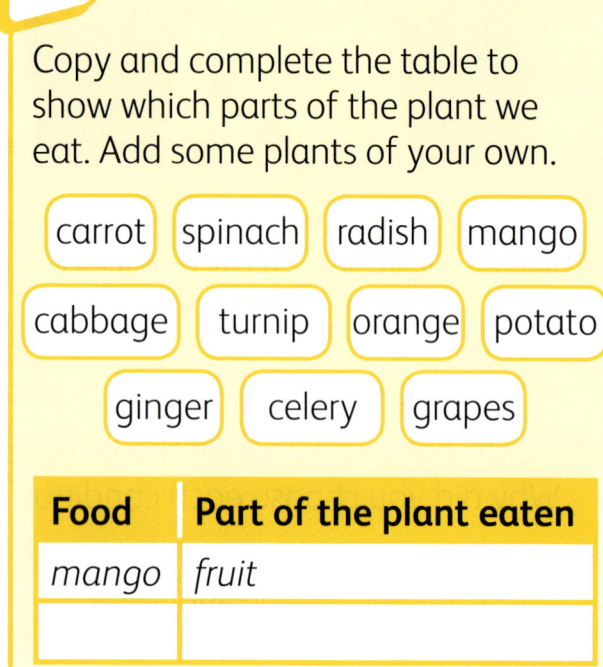

1

Copy and complete the table to show which parts of the plant we eat. Add some plants of your own.

carrot   spinach   radish   mango
cabbage   turnip   orange   potato
ginger   celery   grapes

Food	Part of the plant eaten
mango	fruit

26

What have you learnt about plants?

1

Use these words to complete the sentences below.

seeds | water | nutrients | anchor

supports | warmth | transports | stem

sunlight | make food | collect sunlight | roots | leaves

a All plants have _____, a _____, and _____.

b Plants are grown from _____, which germinate in the correct conditions.

c All plants need _____, _____ and _____ to grow well.

d The roots _____ the plant into the ground and transport _____ and water.

e The stem _____ nutrients and water to the leaves and _____ the plant.

f The leaves _____ and _____ for the plant.

What can you remember?

You have been learning all about plants. Can you:
- ✔ name the four main parts of a plant?
- ✔ explain the function of the leaves?
- ✔ explain three conditions that plants need to grow well?
- ✔ explain how water is taken into a plant?
- ✔ explain how water is transported through the plant?
- ✔ explain how temperature affects a plant's growth?
- ✔ explain what may happen if a plant had damaged roots and stem?

Unit 2 Life processes

⟳ What is living?

Talk partners: Talk to a partner and share what you know about **living** things. For example, living things can ...

Scientific words
living
non-living
nutrition
reproduction
life processes
grow

1

How much do you know already about living things?

a Look at the pictures. Decide if they are living or **non-living** things.

b Copy and complete the table below for each object. Remember to give a reason why you say so for your ideas.

Object	Living	Not living	Not sure	Why?
wooden spoon				

Think like a scientist!

All living things grow. They eat and drink – this is called **nutrition**. They move. They have young – this is called **reproduction**. These are the **life processes**.

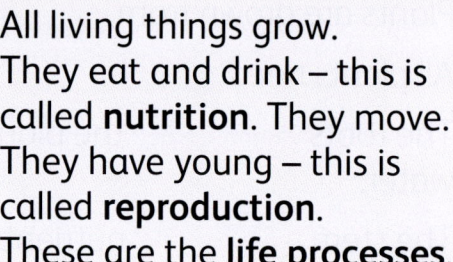

Hint: Can all the things in the pictures **grow**?

Challenge yourself!

Are there other things that we need in order to live? Write down your ideas and reasons. Then share them with the class.

28

Life processes

What living things do

1

The pictures show living things. There are many different types of living things.

a Discuss each living thing with a partner. Talk about why we **classify** (group) things as living.

b Write a sentence to explain why each thing is living.

Challenge yourself!

Blue whales are huge. Some people say that they are the largest animals ever on Earth. They can grow to 30 metres long and can weigh more than 181 metric tons. Just its **tongue** can weigh the same as an elephant!

a Do some research to find a fascinating fact about a life process of another animal. Your fact could be about nutrition, **movement**, growth or reproduction.

b Create a 'Fact file' about it. Try to use some of the words from the scientific words box.

c Share your information with the class.

Scientific words
classify
tongue
movement

Hint: Look back at page 28 to see what all living things do!

29

Unit 2 Life processes

The life processes

Think like a scientist!

You have learnt that all living things can carry out the life processes. Here is a summary of four of the life processes:

movement – all living things move

reproduction – all living things have young like themselves

nutrition – all living things need food and water

growth – all living things grow

1

Match the phrases to the life processes in the boxes:

a taking in food

b increasing in size

c going from one place to another place

d producing new animals.

movement

reproduction

nutrition

growth

2

Can you remember all the life processes?

a Close this book. Write down the four processes you have just learnt.

b Choose an animal. Draw a picture of the animal doing each life process.

30

Life processes

Identifying a living thing

Think like a scientist!

Does the thing in the picture look like a living thing? Sometimes you cannot tell! You can find out by asking questions about the life processes.

Sami showed Ajay the picture above. Sami asked these questions to find out if it is a living thing.

Ajay: Does it move?
Sami: Yes.
Ajay: Does it eat?
Sami: Yes.
Ajay: Can it have babies?
Sami: Yes.
Ajay: Does it grow?
Sami: Yes.
Ajay: Then it is a living thing!
Sami: Yes, it is a pufferfish.

1

Do some research to find out about the pufferfish.

Copy and complete this table. Answer the questions to show what you have found out about the life processes of a pufferfish.

Life process	Question	Answer
reproduction	Does it have babies?	
movement	How does it move?	
growth	How does it grow?	
nutrition	What does it eat?	

Talk partners

Find a picture of an unusual living or non-living thing in your country. Ask a partner to ask you questions about it. Your partner should use the life processes to find out if it is living or non-living. Swap and repeat. Challenge your partner by choosing unusual things!

Unit 2 Life processes

Alive, not alive or never been alive

Think like a scientist!

No living thing lives forever! The amount of time a living thing is **alive** is called its **life span**. Some animals and plants live a long time. They have a long life span. Other animals and plants have a short life span.

1

a Sort the things into three groups: alive, not alive, **never been alive**.

b Make your own list of things in these three groups.

Hint: Ask yourself – does each object have, or did it once have, or carry out, any of the life processes?

Scientific words
alive
life span
never been alive

Did you know?

Greenland sharks have a life span of over 200 years! Their flesh (meat) is poisonous to eat! Maybe that is why they live so long?

Life processes

Movement

Think like a scientist!

Animals move from place to place for different reasons. They move to find food or water, or to find a place to live. Sometimes they move to avoid danger.

Some examples of movement are when animals and humans run, jump, swim, fly and crawl.

Animals can also move in others ways. For example, some beetles roll. Some spiders move by **kiting** or ballooning. To do this, the spider climbs as high as it can. Then it produces silk threads in the air and uses these to travel on the wind. Look at the picture.

1

How do you move each day? Make a list of all the types of movements you made today. Start from when you woke up. Write reasons for why you moved.

2

How do these animals move?

a Match each word in the boxes to the animals below, to show how it moves. Do some animals move in more than one way?

swim   jump   run   fly

b Choose two of the animals below. Write three reasons why each animal might move.

cheetah

bird

fish

cricket

Scientific word
kiting

33

Unit 2 Life processes

 # Reasons for movement

1

Can you remember the life processes?

a Make a list of the life processes.

b Look at the box below. Which are good reasons for animals moving?

c Which are not good reasons?

d Explain your answers to a partner.
Try to use your list of life processes in your answers.

1 to find food
2 for a change
3 to keep warm
4 to find a mate
5 because it is Tuesday
6 to find water
7 to find a place to live
8 to hide
9 to avoid (stay away from) animals that might want to eat them.

orangutans

Think like a scientist!

Humans and animals can move in more than one way. You had to learn how to move. You probably started to move by rolling. Then you moved by crawling, and then by walking. Finally you learnt to jump, hop, skip and run. Perhaps you can swim or move in other ways? However, one way humans cannot move is by flying – unless you are in a plane or other machine that can move for you!

Life processes

Growing

Think like a scientist!

All animals start as young. We call human young, babies. Babies are small and must be looked after because they cannot look after themselves.

Not all young animals are looked after. Snakes look after themselves from birth.

1

Create a 'Memory box' to show the ways you have grown since you were a baby. Include photographs, drawings and writing, special objects or a toy from when you were a baby. Think about these things:

- How big were you as a baby?
- What could you do then, compared to what you can do now?
- What kind of food did you have when you were born, compared to now?
- How old were you when you began to talk?
- When did you start to walk?

What would happen if people never stopped growing? What would be good about it? What would be bad about never stopping growing?

Talk partners

Share your memory box with a partner. What things do you both have? What things show that you have grown?

35

Unit 2 Life processes

Predicting growth

1

Ananya was looking at her family's photo album. She noticed that every year she was taller. She wondered if she could predict how tall she might grow. Ananya hoped to be tall enough to play for the basketball team. Everyone in this year's team is more than 141 cm tall.

The **bar chart** shows Ananya's **height** from ages 2 to 7 years. It also shows the average (most common) height for girls of each age. Answer the questions below:

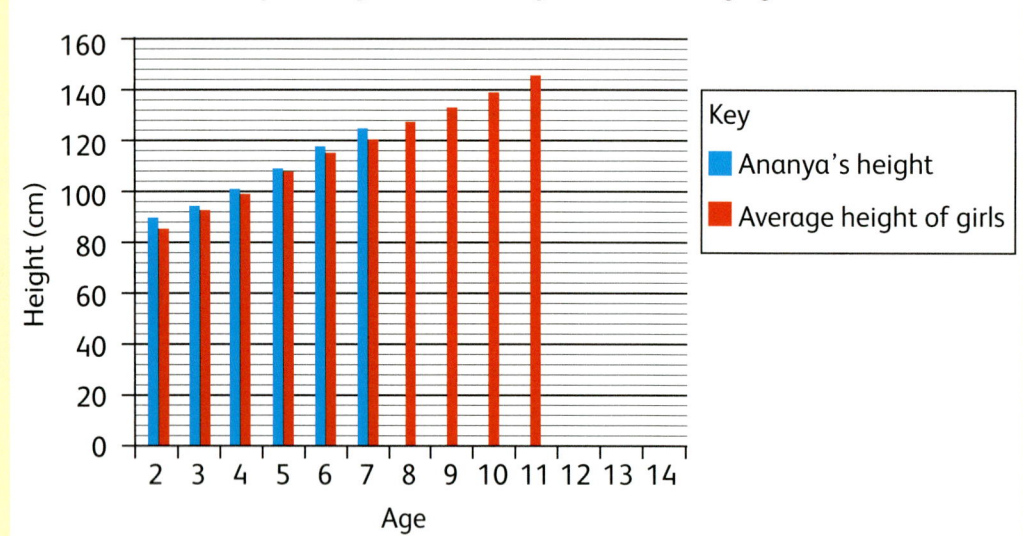

a What happens to Ananya's height as she gets older?

b Is Ananya a tall or short girl?

c Use the information on the bar chart to predict Ananya's height at 10 years, 12 years and 14 years old.

d Write a letter to Ananya. Using your prediction, explain whether you think she will or will not be tall enough to play basketball for the school team.

Hint: Compare her height to the average height of girls.

Scientific words
bar chart
height

Life processes

Nutrition in humans

Think like a scientist!

Nutrition is getting the right foods for health and growth. Living things need food to grow, reproduce and move. Food provides the **energy** that keeps living things moving! Living things need a variety of different foods for proper growth and **repair**. Eating the right foods helps the body to get better quicker after being ill or injured. Animals get their foods from plants or other animals.

Scientific words
energy
repair
fruits

Sammy only ate white foods. He would not eat any **fruits** or vegetables. He would not eat brown meat. He ate the same things every day. This worried Sammy's mother. She thought Sammy would become ill.

Talk partners

Talk to a partner. Should Sammy's mother be worried about him? Why?

1

Answer these questions.

a Why do humans and animals need nutrition?

b Write down what you had for breakfast. Did the foods come from plants or animals?

c What is your favourite food? Why?

d What do you think would happen if you only ever ate your favourite food?

e What would happen if you had nothing to eat? Use words from the scientific words box (and others) to explain your answer.

37

Unit 2 Life processes

Nutrition in animals

Think like a scientist!

Animals and plants need food and water (nutrition) to stay alive. Plants make their own food. Animals must find food. Different animals feed on (eat) different foods. The foods include grass, seeds, nuts, fruits, leaves and other animals, including insects, fish and birds.

Some animals eat only one type of food. For example, the giant panda only eats bamboo shoots.

giant panda eating bamboo

Animals such as goats eat many types of plants. They eat things like leaves, grass, vegetables and even flowers. Some animals eat other animals. Frogs, for example, feed on flies and insects.

Some animals eat plants and animals. The two-toed sloth, for example, eats leaves, fruits, slow-moving animals and bird's eggs. Humans also eat plants and animals.

two-toed sloth

1

Select an animal and research what the animal eats.

a Does it eat plants, animals or both?

b Find out about how the animal moves.

c Present your research in a booklet (mini-book).

Do you know what a herbivore, carnivore and omnivore are?

38

Life processes

Hibernation

Scientific words
hibernation
dormant
drought

Think like a scientist!

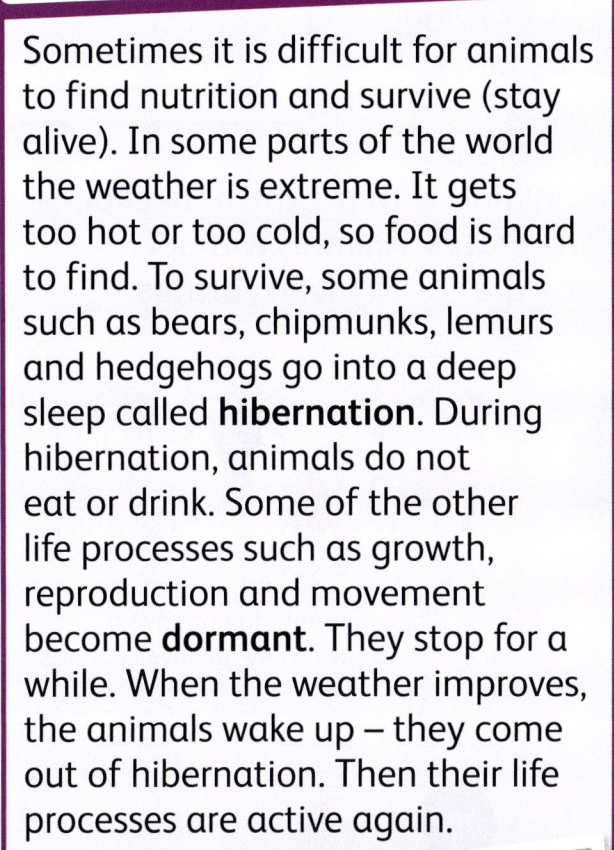

Sometimes it is difficult for animals to find nutrition and survive (stay alive). In some parts of the world the weather is extreme. It gets too hot or too cold, so food is hard to find. To survive, some animals such as bears, chipmunks, lemurs and hedgehogs go into a deep sleep called **hibernation**. During hibernation, animals do not eat or drink. Some of the other life processes such as growth, reproduction and movement become **dormant**. They stop for a while. When the weather improves, the animals wake up – they come out of hibernation. Then their life processes are active again.

1

a Research an animal that hibernates. Create a 'Fact file' about the animal. Use the scientific words when writing your facts. Use these questions to help you:
 - What time of year does the animal hibernate? Why?
 - What part of the world does it live in?
 - How does it prepare for hibernation?
 - Where does it hibernate?
 - What happens to its life processes during hibernation?
 - When does it wake up, and why?

b Present your fact file to the class or a small group.

Did you know?

The fat-tailed dwarf lemur lives in Madagascar, Africa. It hibernates for seven months of the year! This lemur does not hibernate to avoid very cold temperatures. It hibernates to avoid **drought**. During a drought, food is scarce – there is hardly any – because the land is so dry.

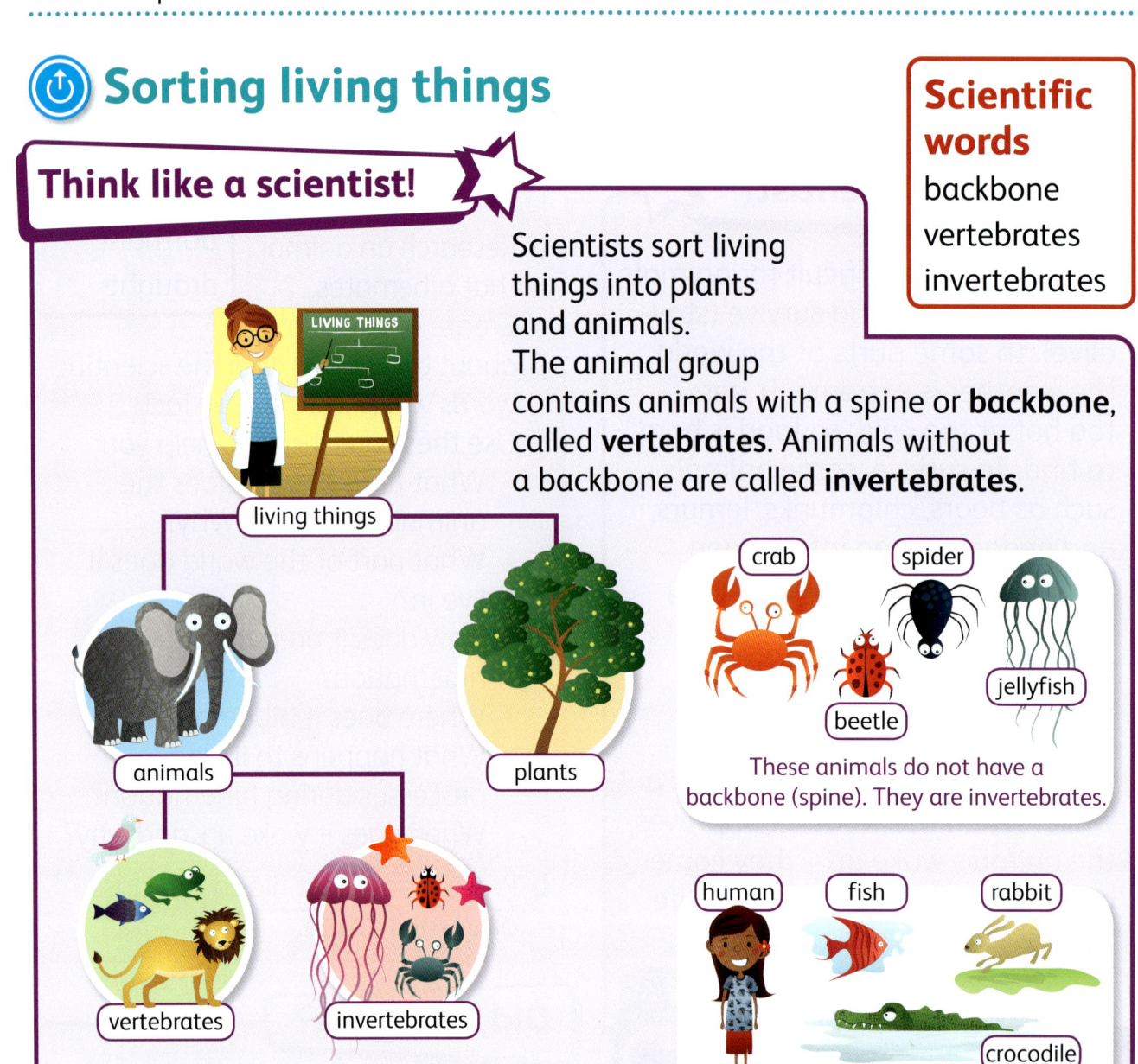

Unit 2 Life processes

Sorting living things

Think like a scientist!

Scientists sort living things into plants and animals. The animal group contains animals with a spine or **backbone**, called **vertebrates**. Animals without a backbone are called **invertebrates**.

Scientific words
backbone
vertebrates
invertebrates

living things
- animals
  - vertebrates
  - invertebrates
- plants

crab, spider, jellyfish, beetle

These animals do not have a backbone (spine). They are invertebrates.

human, fish, rabbit, crocodile

These animals have a spine. They are vertebrates.

1

snail   snake   frog   starfish
monkey   toucan   tiger   lobster

Do some research about these animals. Find out which group they belong to. Sort them into vertebrates or invertebrates.

Challenge yourself!

Draw a sorting diagram of living things. **Hint:** look at the one above. Add some plants and animals (vertebrates and invertebrates) that live in your country.

Life processes

Sorting vertebrates

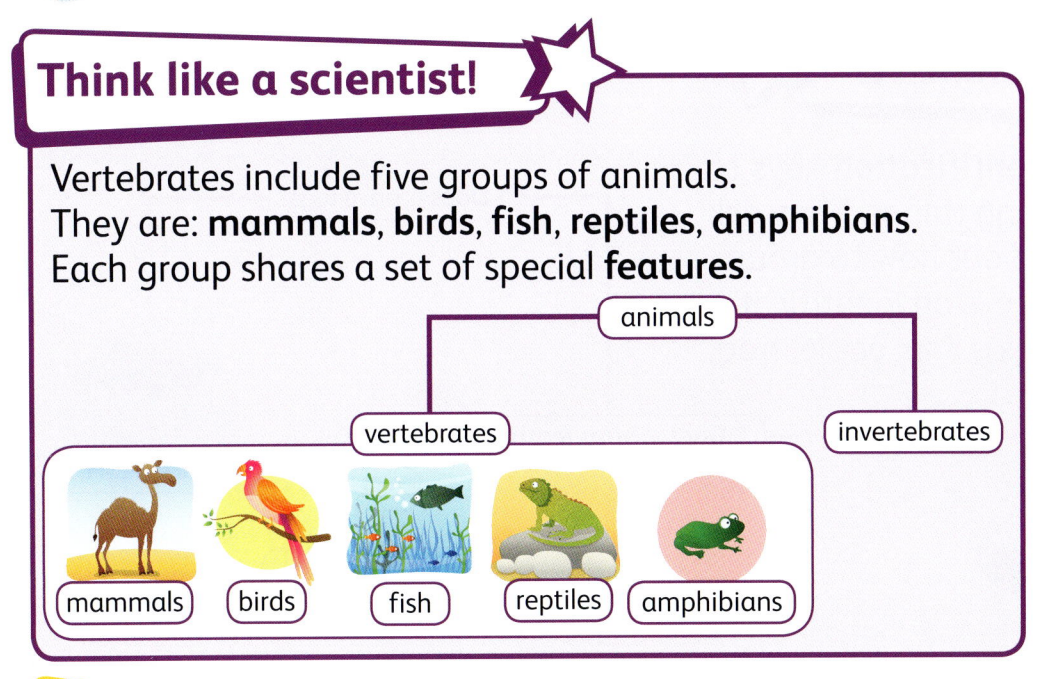

Think like a scientist!

Vertebrates include five groups of animals.
They are: **mammals**, **birds**, **fish**, **reptiles**, **amphibians**.
Each group shares a set of special **features**.

animals → vertebrates, invertebrates

vertebrates: mammals, birds, fish, reptiles, amphibians

Scientific words
mammals
birds
fish
reptiles
amphibians
features
skin
breathe
lungs
gills

1

Research the features of each vertebrate group.
What do the animals in each group have in common?

a Copy and complete the table to show your ideas. The first group, mammals, has been done for you. Add the headings Birds, Fish, Reptiles and Amphibians in the other four columns of your table.

b As you find out more about each animal group, add the facts to your table.

Questions about features	Mammals				
Where do the young come from?	*young grow in mother's body and are born*				
What is their body covering? (fur, feathers, scales, **skin**)	*fur or skin*				
How do they move?	*on four or two legs*				
What types of foods do they eat?	*plants and other animals*				
How do they **breathe**? (**lungs** or **gills**?)	*by using lungs*				

41

Unit 2 Life processes

Classifying using identification keys

Think like a scientist!

Scientists use **identification keys** to classify (sort) living things. They ask questions to find out how to group living things. Here is an identification key that classifies a lion, eagle, frog, lizard and shark.

1 Does it have legs?
- YES
- NO → shark (FISH)

2 Does it have feathers?
- YES → eagle (BIRD)
- NO

3 Does it lay eggs?
- YES
- NO → lion (MAMMAL)

4 ?
- YES → lizard (REPTILE)
- NO → frog (AMPHIBIAN)

1

Look at the identification key above.

a What should question 4 be to separate the lizard from the frog? You may need to do some research first to find out their special features.

b Think of a different set of questions to sort the animals. Use them to create your own identification key to classify the animals. The final line should show which group the vertebrate belongs to – mammal, bird, reptile, fish or amphibian.

c Choose some vertebrates from your country. Create another identification key.

Look back at your work from page 41 for a reminder of the five vertebrate groups and their special features.

Scientific word
identification keys

Life processes

Reproduction

Think like a scientist!

Reproduction is the process by which living things produce young, called **offspring**. Some animals lay eggs to reproduce. Some animals have babies called live young.

Vertebrates:
- Mammals have live young that look the same as the adults (just smaller). The live young grow into adults.
- Birds, fish, amphibians and reptiles lay eggs. The young continue to develop inside the eggs. Most eggs hatch young that look like tiny adults. After hatching, the young grow into adults.
- Some amphibians such as frogs are different. After hatching, the young go through several stages – called **metamorphosis** – before they look like the adult.

Invertebrates:
- Invertebrates such as dragonflies lay eggs, but sometimes the young do not look like the adults when they hatch. The young also go through metamorphosis before they become an adult.
- Not all invertebrates go through metamorphosis, for example, snails lay eggs, but these hatch into mini snails.

frog

1

Write whether each living thing below has live young or lays eggs to reproduce. First do some research. Find out if each animal is a mammal, bird, fish, reptile, amphibian or invertebrate. The first one has been done for you. Do any of these animals go through metamorphosis?

a *cat – vertebrate: mammal – live young*

b salamander   c snake   d parrot
e spider   f goldfish   g mouse
h giraffe   i butterfly   j antelope
k alligator   l shark

Scientific words
offspring
metamorphosis

43

Unit 2 Life processes

Life cycles

Think like a scientist!

A **life cycle** is a diagram that shows the main stages of the life of an **organism** (a living thing).

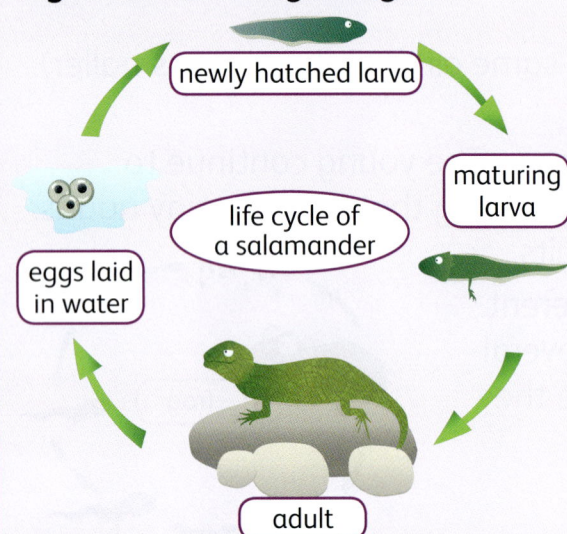

life cycle of a salamander: eggs laid in water → newly hatched larva → maturing larva → adult

Scientists make models that help to explain ideas such as the life cycle. The cycle is used to show what happens (for example, in the life of a plant or animal). Not all animals have simple life cycles.

1

Labels: adult, larva, moult, eggs

Put the life cycle of a dragonfly (an invertebrate) in the right order.

Hint: A **moult** is when the dragonfly sheds its skin to reveal a new skin. A **larva** is used to describe a young dragonfly.

Challenge yourself!

Choose an animal that interests you and research it. Then make a scientific model of the animal's life cycle. Present your findings to the class or a small group.

When you have finished your life cycle model, swap it with a partner. Look at each other's life cycle model. Then give each other a helpful comment to improve the model. Make changes to your work.

Scientific words
life cycle
organism
moult
larva

Life processes

What have you learnt about life processes?

1

Choose the correct words to match each statement.

- nutrition
- reproduction
- growth
- movement

a Moving
b Changing in size as it gets older
c Food and water needed for living
d Having babies like the parents

2

True or False?

a Invertebrates have a backbone.
b Some life processes become dormant during hibernation.
c A lifespan is the amount of time a living thing is alive.
d A moult is when a dragonfly sheds its tail.

What can you remember?

You have been learning about life processes. Can you:
- ✓ name four life processes found in humans and animals?
- ✓ describe the differences between living and non-living things using the life processes?
- ✓ explain why nutrition is important for animals?
- ✓ list three reasons why animals move?
- ✓ explain the life cycle of a human?
- ✓ explain the difference between a living and a non-living thing?
- ✓ explain what reproduction means?
- ✓ sort animals into groups and explain why?

45

Unit 3 Keeping healthy

What do you know about keeping healthy?

1

Look at the pictures of a learner doing different activities.
Which activities are **healthy**?
Which activities are less healthy?

a   b 
c    d 
e    f

Think like a scientist!

There are many ways to stay healthy. Watching some television is fine. But spending all day sitting in front of a television screen is less healthy. To stay healthy you need to:
- eat the right foods
- drink lots of water
- get enough **exercise**.

How are the learners in the photographs above being healthy or less healthy?

Talk partners

Talk about the pictures in Activity 1 with a partner. Do you agree on which activities show a healthy lifestyle and which show a less healthy lifestyle? Why?

Scientific words
healthy
exercise

2

Draw pictures of other healthy and less healthy activities.

Keeping healthy

Favourite foods

1 Draw your favourite meal. Label each food in the meal. When do you eat this meal?

What is your favourite meal?

Think like a scientist!

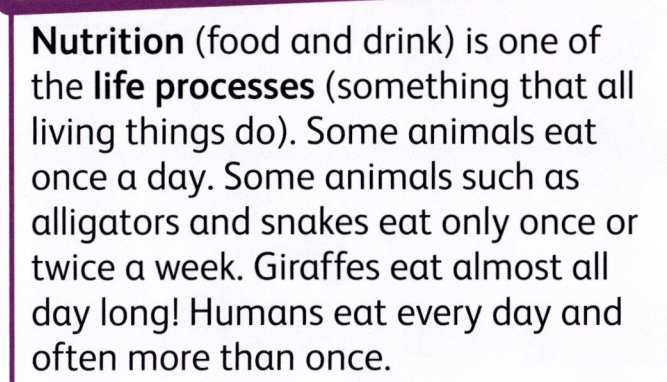

Nutrition (food and drink) is one of the **life processes** (something that all living things do). Some animals eat once a day. Some animals such as alligators and snakes eat only once or twice a week. Giraffes eat almost all day long! Humans eat every day and often more than once.

We eat to give us **energy** to live and grow, to move and to think. You eat different things now than when you were a baby. Food is our fuel. What we eat every day is called our **diet**.

2 Here is Tsige's lunchbox.

a Are all the items healthy choices?

b Change three foods to make her choices healthier. Give a reason for each change.

Scientific words
nutrition
life processes
energy
diet

47

Unit 3 Keeping healthy

A balanced diet

Think like a scientist!

Humans need to eat a **range** of foods to have a **balanced diet**. A balanced diet means eating a variety (different types) of foods – not the same foods every day. Different types of foods have different uses for the body. Food helps the body to grow, move, maintain (care for) and repair itself. The dinner plate shows the different **food groups** and how much of each of these food group we should eat each day.

The sizes of the food groups on this dinner plate show a balanced diet.

1. dairy produce
2. fresh vegetables and fruits
3. starchy foods such as pasta, rice, potatoes and bread
4. high protein foods such as meat, pulses and eggs
5. high fat or high sugar foods

1 Look at the size of each food group on the dinner plate above.

a Which food groups are the biggest? Do some research to find out why.

b Which food group is the smallest? Do some research to find out why.

2 Felix found an orange and a chocolate bar in his lunchbox. He told his friend Irina that the orange was healthy and the chocolate bar was unhealthy. Irina said that one chocolate bar was not unhealthy.

Look again at the dinner plate above. Who do you think is right? Why? Remember to give a reason for your answer.

Scientific words
range
balanced diet
food groups

48

Keeping healthy

⏻ Healthy eating traffic lights

Think like a scientist!

Red-light foods are high in **fat** and high in **sugar**. When you see them, make a different choice, or just have a very small amount. Foods that are high in fat and sugar can be bad for your health.

Yellow-light foods are for growth and repair. They help your body to get better or mend when you are ill or injure yourself.
You may eat these foods at every meal but in small portions.

Green-light foods give you energy. They also make sure that your body works well. They contain the **minerals** and **vitamins** that we need for a healthy life. These foods should make up the biggest part of every meal.

Why is it also important to drink plenty of clean water during the day to stay healthy?

Scientific words
fat
sugar
minerals
vitamins
sweet

1

Look at the two lunchboxes. Then answer the questions.

a Classify (sort) the green, yellow and red foods in each lunchbox.

b Do either of the packed lunches have examples of all three types of the traffic light foods? Are they balanced?

c Mix the foods in the lunchboxes. Make new, more balanced lunchboxes.

egg   **sweet**
cheese   chicken
starfruit banana
grapes   carrots

lollipops crisps
sweets   sandwich
cupcakes   soda

49

Unit 3 Keeping healthy

Vitamins and minerals

Think like a scientist!

Vitamins and minerals help your body to function correctly. Your body must be able to move, grow, maintain (care for) and repair itself.

Your body gets vitamins and minerals from the foods you eat each day. Some foods have more vitamins and minerals than others.

Vitamins and minerals come from plant or animal foods. Look back at the plate of how much of the different foods to eat on page 48.

Foods such as tomatoes and broccoli contain plenty of vitamins and minerals.

Challenge yourself!

Food packaging usually has a label to show its **nutritional information** (about the nutrients in the food). Collect different food packaging and look for the nutritional information labels.

a Make a list of the vitamins and minerals on the nutritional information labels.

b What **units of measure** are used for vitamins and minerals?

c Choose one vitamin and one mineral. Research how they help your body to work.

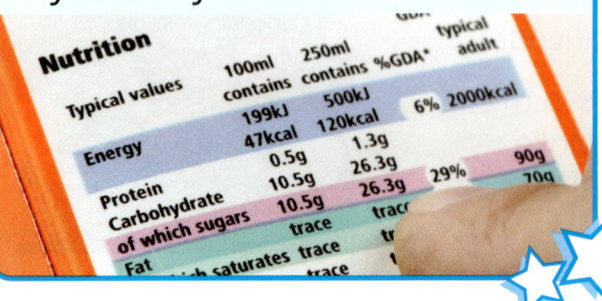

Some vitamins and minerals may help with more than one body function!

1

Design, draw and label a recipe that is rich in vitamins and minerals.

a Research the vitamins and minerals in your ingredients. Draw and label your recipe.

b Prepare your recipe and try it. Do you like the taste? How could you improve it?

Scientific words
nutritional information
units of measure

Keeping healthy

What happens to the body without vitamins?

Think like a scientist!

Long ago, sailors spent many months at sea while exploring the world. During the journey they often became ill with **scurvy**. Scurvy causes **skin** sores and difficulty in **breathing**. Bones can change shape and teeth can fall out! The **rations** (food supplies) that the sailors ate had too few vitamins and minerals. This caused scurvy.

Even longer ago, Chinese sailors took fresh ginger to sea with them. Eating fresh ginger prevented scurvy.
European sailors did not take any ginger and became ill.

In 1747, a scientist named James Lind carried out a test on 12 sailors with scurvy. He gave each pair of sailors extra food, as well as their rations. Look at his table of results. The test lasted only six days. By then, he had used all the lemons and oranges on the ship.

Sailors	Extra food	After six days
1 and 2	a quart of apple drink (about 1 litre)	some improvement
3 and 4	ginger and cinnamon drink	no change
5 and 6	seawater	no change
7 and 8	lemons and oranges	total recovery
9 and 10	mustard and horseradish	no change
11 and 12	a teaspoon of vinegar	no change

1

Look at the table of results of the tests.
a Do you think the test was fair?
b Which sailors got better? Why do you think this was?
c Which sailors did not get better? Why?
d What do you think James Lind suggested would be the best way to cure scurvy? Why?

Scientific words
scurvy
skin
breathing
rations

51

Unit 3 Keeping healthy

A cure for scurvy

Think like a scientist!

James Lind's work is one of the first examples of a scientific test. His results were not taken seriously for another 40 years. By this time, more than 100,000 sailors had died of scurvy. In 1800, ships kept limes on board because they were easier to buy than lemons. Every sailor got lime juice.

Sailors knew that they needed citrus **fruits** (oranges, lemons, limes) or green vegetables (such as **sea kale**) to stay healthy at sea. However, they were not sure why. In 1928, two scientists discovered that it was the **vitamin C** in the fruits and vegetables that prevented scurvy.

1

The table shows the amounts of vitamin C per 100 grams in each item. The higher the number the more vitamin C the item contains.

Fruit or vegetable	Mg of vitamin C per 100 g
ginger	5
limes	29
lemons	53
oranges	53
sea kale	120
apple drink	4

a What has the most vitamin C?

b Think back to page 51. Why was there only 'some improvement' when sailors drank apple juice compared to 'total recovery' when they ate lemons and oranges?

Scientific words
fruits
sea kale
vitamin C

Pretend that you are the captain of a ship. Which fruit would you take on a very long journey at sea?

Did you know?

Sea kale was called 'scurvy grass' by sailors in the 1700s. This was because sailors felt better when they ate it! Sea kale is often found near the seashore.

sea kale

Keeping healthy

Energy and kilojoules

Think like a scientist!

Scientific word
kilojoules

Food and water help us to move, grow and repair our bodies. We measure the amount of energy in food in **kilojoules**. Different foods have different numbers of kilojoules. Some foods such as fish help the body to repair and grow. Other foods such as pasta release energy slowly.

Different people need different types and amounts of foods to stay healthy. Athletes may use huge amounts of energy during training – so must eat many kilojoules. Someone who exercises very little will not need so many.

1

These menu cards show what three people eat in a day.

ATHLETE

★ ENERGY ★
about 23,000 kilojoules a day

Breakfast – ackee and saltfish with dumplings, cooked banana, yellow yam and potato
Lunch – pasta and chicken breast
Dinner – rice and peas with meat
Snacks – chicken nuggets and chips

GRANDMOTHER

★ ENERGY ★
6700 kilojoules a day

Breakfast – yoghurt with muesli and berries
Lunch – vegetable quesadilla on a wholewheat tortilla
Dinner – grilled salmon with spicy salsa, a chocolate bar
Snacks – almond nuts, biscuits

GIRL

★ ENERGY ★
about 6700 kilojoules a day

Breakfast – breakfast cereal
Lunch – cheese sandwich, crisps, an apple, a chocolate bar
Dinner – pizza and ice cream
Snacks – chicken nuggets and chips

a Compare the foods that the athlete, the girl and her grandmother eat. Which menu cards show the most balanced diet? Why? Use the traffic light system on page 49 to help you.

b Which menu card could be healthier? How?

c Why does the athlete need more food than the grandmother?

d The girl and her grandmother eat the same number of kilojoules per day. Which menu card provides the best types of foods for energy? Why?

Unit 3 Keeping healthy

The right fuel

Think like a scientist!

Remember, the energy your body needs to function comes from the food you eat. Food is the fuel for our body!

The unit of measure for the energy in food is kilojoules. If you are very active, you use more energy, so you may need to eat more kilojoules. If you are less active, you will use less energy, so you may need to eat fewer kilojoules.

energy used

energy used

If you eat the same number of kilojoules that your body needs, you will stay healthy. However, you need to choose the fuel for your body carefully! Some foods such as doughnuts contain one-quarter of all the kilojoules a body needs for a whole day. They are not a good **source** of energy or fuel. They are high in sugar and fat, which can damage your health. Doughnuts are red-light foods.

doughnuts

1

Think about what you have learnt about foods. Then create a menu for a football player and a menu for a school teacher. Will they need the same types of foods for fuel? Will they use the same amount of energy in a day?

Scientific word
source

Keeping healthy

Food and health benefits

Scientific words

health benefit

Think like a scientist!

A **health benefit** is something that is good for your body. Some foods are better for your body than others. Some types of foods have few health benefits. We should try not to eat these foods too often. If we do eat foods with few health benefits, we should only eat them in small amounts.

1

Look at the foods in the pictures. Decide if each one is:
- a food with few health benefits to the body
- a food with many health benefits for the body

Give a reason for each answer.

- glass of milk
- chicken salad 
- fizzy drink 
- chocolates 
- fish curry and rice 
- sweets 
- cheese and tomato pizza 

Challenge yourself!

Some foods are called 'superfoods'. Black beans, kale, avocado, amaranth and kohlrabi are some examples of superfoods.

a Find out what 'superfoods' means.

b Do you, or does someone you know eat any superfoods? Make a list. Find out what health benefits these superfoods provide.

2

Create a poster to explain why it is important to eat healthily. Include some foods that you should eat in a balanced diet. Add your findings on superfoods.

Unit 3 Keeping healthy

Health facts and fiction

Think like a scientist!

There are many ideas about health and food. Some of these ideas are fact (true). Some are fiction (false)! Have you heard any of these statements before?

Eating chicken soup will cure a cold.

Not true and not false. It is not possible to cure a common cold. Eating chicken soup can help the body to fight the **effects** of the cold. The nutrients in chicken soup can help the body to get better.

Carrots are good for your eyesight.

True. Carrots contain vitamin A. This is needed for healthy **sight**.

Healthy people need to take vitamin and mineral tablets.

False. If you eat a balanced diet, your body will get all it needs without tablets. You will only need vitamin and mineral tablets if your body is short of a certain vitamin or mineral. A doctor can tell you if this has happened.

1

Research one of these statements to find out if it is True or False.

- Eating bread crusts makes your hair curl.
- Fish is a brain food.
- Eating too much chocolate makes learners overactive.

Challenge yourself!

Some scientists think that learners who eat breakfast score better in tests than learners who do not eat breakfast.
Why might this be true?
Design a healthy breakfast.

Scientific words
sight   effects

56

Keeping healthy

Active and inactive

Think like a scientist!

When you run, skip, hop, dance, play football or other sport, you are exercising. This is called being active.
Being active makes and keeps your body strong and healthy.
You have many **muscles** in your body.
The most important muscle is your **heart**.
Being active will help to keep your heart healthy.

1
a
b
c
d
e
f

Look at the activities in the pictures.
Sort them into an activity list –
from very active to inactive
(opposite of active).

very active —— active —— inactive

2

Some people like to play tennis.
Some people like to paddle a canoe.
What is your favourite exercise?
How does it keep you healthy?
Use the words in the scientific words box in your answers.

Scientific words
muscles
heart

57

Unit 3 Keeping healthy

How Sami spends a day

1

Sami recorded what he did for a day. He made a **bar chart** to show the results.

a Which activity takes up most of the day?

b Which activity does Sami do for the shortest amount of time?

c Which activity could Sami do less of or swap for a healthier activity?

d Do you think Sami is leading a healthy lifestyle? Why?

e How could he make his lifestyle healthier?

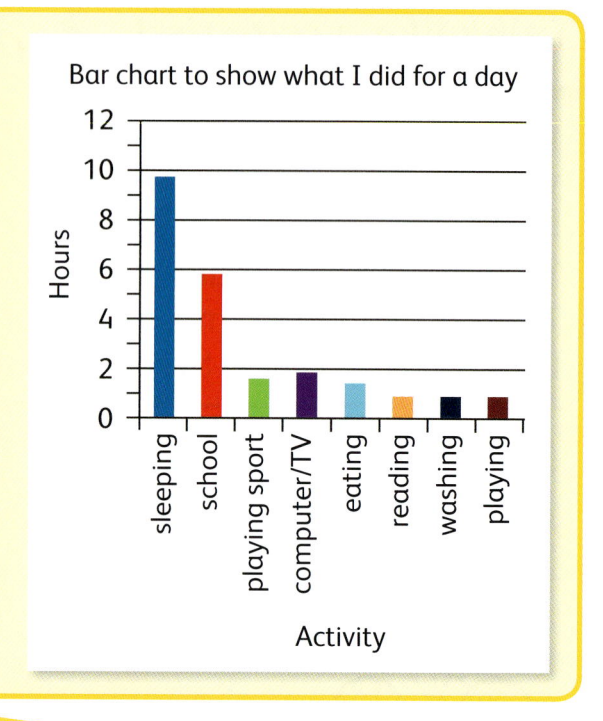

Bar chart to show what I did for a day

Think like a scientist!

An eight-year-old should sleep for about 11 hours each night.
Sleep is as important as healthy eating and exercise.
Learners who do not get enough sleep are less likely to be healthy.

2

Create a list of what you do each day.

a Compare your list to Sami's. What is the same? What is different?

b Think of one thing that you will try to do to make your life healthier.

c Create a bar chart like Sami's to show the results of your day.

What is a healthy lifestyle?

Scientific word
bar chart

58

Keeping healthy

Screen time and health

Think like a scientist!

Scientists have found that too much screen time can be less healthy. This includes watching television, playing computer games (or looking at your phone). Too much time spent on these activities can increase the chance of being ill or less healthy. Screen time itself is not bad. It is just that while doing these activities, people do not move around much. They are inactive.

1

Sami, Ajay, Gabriella and Mateo recorded how much time they spent watching television and playing computer games on a weekend day.

Bar chart to show time spent watching television or playing computer games in one day

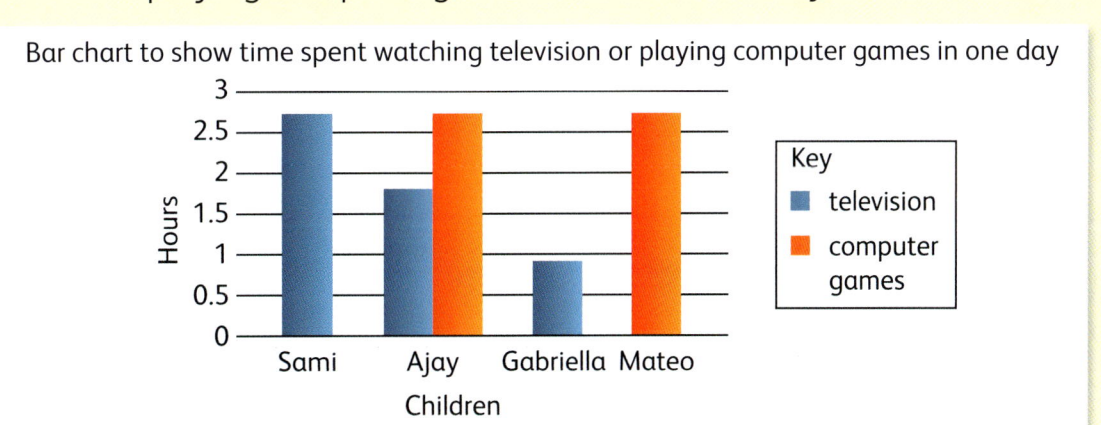

Key: television, computer games

a Who did not watch television that day?
b Who was the most inactive?
c Who watched the most television?
d Who played computer games the least?
e Who sat in front of a computer or a television for the most time?
f How could Ajay change his day to become more active?
g What could Sami and Mateo do to become more active?

Who are you most like – Sami, Ajay, Gabriella or Mateo?

Unit 3 Keeping healthy

Keeping your heart healthy

Think like a scientist!

Scientific word
heartbeat

The heart is a muscle. It works hard at pumping your blood around your body. You can feel your **heartbeat**. Place your hand on the upper left-hand side of your chest. You can make your heart stronger: do exercises that make you breathe more often. This makes your heart beat faster.

1

Activity	Effect on the heartbeat
watching TV	♥
swimming	♥♥♥
walking	♥♥
reading a book	♥
playing a computer game	♥
playing basketball	♥♥♥

Key
♥ normal heartbeat
♥♥ slightly faster heartbeat
♥♥♥ much faster heartbeat

Gideon drew up the table above to show the activities he tried and how they affected his heartbeat. Some activities had no effect on his normal heartbeat. Other activities made his heart beat faster. He tested this by placing a hand on his chest (to feel his heart beat) after doing each activity.

a Which activities had little effect on his heartbeat? Why?

b Which activities were best for exercising Gideon's heart? Why?

c What other exercises would you include to exercise Gideon's heart? Why?

d Try some of these activities and draw up a table of your results. Use a key to identify the results of your activities the way Gideon did.

Keeping healthy

Heart beat investigation

Think like a scientist!

Scientific words
oxygen
air

On page 60 you found out that when you exercise your heart beats faster. This is because it needs more **oxygen** (**air** that we need to breathe). So you breathe more often in order for more oxygen to get to the heart and muscles.

1

How many breaths do you take in one minute after different exercises?

You will need...
- stopwatch or clock with a second hand

a Plan an investigation to find out. Think about:
- how to measure the number of breaths in each minute
- what types of exercises you will try.

b Predict which exercise will make you breathe more per minute.

c Do your investigation. Then record the results in a table like this.

Activity	Number of breaths per minute
sitting at your desk	
walking slowly for one minute	

d Put your results in a bar chart.

e Which activities had the most breaths per minute? Which do you think were best for exercising the heart muscle? Why?

Be careful

Do not hold your breath! Also check that the place where you are exercising is clear and safe before you start.

61

Unit 3 Keeping healthy

The effect of exercise on breathing

1

Sahara and Fozia tried various exercises for two minutes. They counted the number of breaths they took in one minute after doing these exercises. They kept the person the same to make the test fair. They counted their breaths for exactly the same amount of time. They recorded their results in the bar chart:

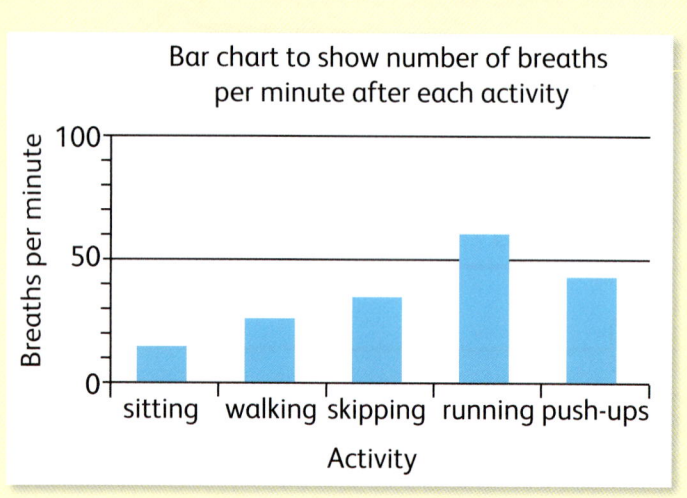

Bar chart to show number of breaths per minute after each activity

a Which activity raised the breathing rate the most?

b Which activity do you think exercises the heart muscle the least?

2

Look at the bar chart in Activity 1. Are these statements True or False?

a The highest number of breaths was when they were walking.

b The lowest number of breaths was when they were sitting.

c They took 60 breaths per minute when they were running.

d They took 10 breaths per minute when they were walking.

e The more vigorous (active) the exercise the greater the number of breaths.

f Your breathing rate will be lower when doing moderate (less active) exercise, than when you do vigorous activities.

Challenge yourself!

Make up some statements that are true and false for your investigation on page 61.

Ask a partner to work out which statement is true and which is false.

Keeping healthy

⏻ Being healthy and happy

Think like a scientist!

Exercise is good for you!
If you have a strong and **flexible** body that you can bend, you will be able to run, jump, skip and do all the sports you like. Exercise is also good for happiness! Scientists have found that people who run and jump are happier than people who do no exercise.

1

Being healthy and happy is the same as saying that you eat well and exercise enough. Your body works well and you feel good. You can also do all the things you want.

To stay healthy, remember these things:
- Eat a balanced diet.
- Drink plenty of water.
- Get enough sleep (at least ten hours).
- Limit the time you spend in front of a screen (television or computer).
- Move around and exercise.

Write an idea for each point above to make them special to you.
For example: *I will try to eat more vegetables. I will eat doughnuts only on special occasions.*

Talk partners

How does exercise make you happy? With a partner, make a list of the health benefits of exercise.

Look back at pages 48 and 49 to remind you about the foods in a balanced diet.

Scientific word
flexible

63

Unit 3 Keeping healthy

Soap, health and hand washing

Think like a scientist!

There are between 10,000 and 10 million **bacteria** (germs) on each hand! Some bacteria are harmless. Some bacteria cause illness.

- Damp hands spread 1000 times more germs than dry hands.
- The number of germs on your fingertips doubles after you use the toilet.
- When you cough, germs can travel about three metres if you do not put your hand or a handkerchief over your nose and mouth. One person can spread almost one million bacteria in one school day.

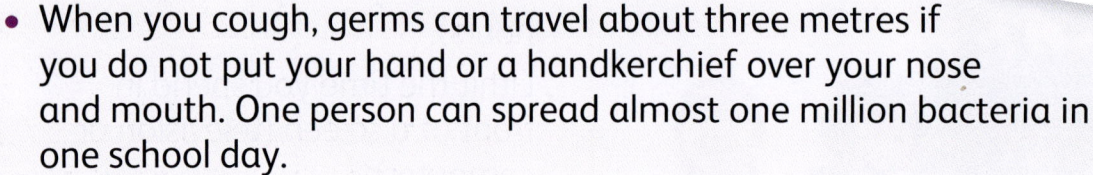

Hand washing is one of the best ways to stop the spread of many types of diseases that cause illnesses. Clean hands can stop bacteria from moving from one person to another and through a whole community.

Did you know?

The amount of time you should spend washing your hands each time is at least 20 seconds. That is about as long as it takes you to sing the 'Happy Birthday' song twice! Try it the next time you wash your hands.

Talk partners

Talk to a partner about when you wash your hands. How often do you wash your hands? After which activities do you wash your hands? Can you think of tasks that you do where you need to wash your hands:
a before?
b after?
c before and after?

Scientific word
bacteria

Keeping healthy

What have you learnt about keeping healthy?

1

naan bread
fizzy drink
chicken curry with rice
baked pineapple

a Look at the pictures above. Do these foods provide a balanced, healthy meal? Why or why not?

b Sort the items into the food groups that you learnt about on the dinner plate on page 48.

c Sort the foods using the traffic light system on page 49.

d Make a suggestion for a food or drink that you could swap for healthier options. Explain your ideas.

2

True or False?

a Learners need to eat the same foods every day.

b Drinking too many sugary drinks is less healthy.

c Learners who are 7 or 8 years old need seven hours of sleep each day.

d Running, jumping, skipping and playing chase are exercise.

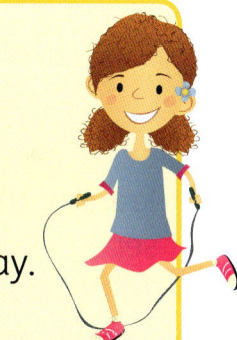

What can you remember?

You have been learning about keeping healthy. Can you:
- ✔ explain what foods are damaging to our health and why?
- ✔ describe a balanced diet?
- ✔ explain why hand washing is so important?
- ✔ say why we need to exercise to stay healthy?
- ✔ explain what changes happen to our body when we exercise?

Unit 4 The senses

The human senses

Think like a scientist!

Our senses are **touch**, **taste**, **smell**, **sight** and **hearing**. The **eyes** sense light (which gives us sight). The nose is where we have our sense of smell. The **skin** senses touch. The ears are for hearing. The **tongue** helps us to taste different things.

Our senses work together with the brain. They get information about the world we live in, where we are and what we are doing. We often use more than one of our senses at the same time.

Talk partners

Pretend that you are only allowed four senses. Which sense would you give up? Talk to your partner about this.
Explain why you made your choice.

1
List the senses. Then draw and write what you like best about each sense.

Did you know?

Your back is one of the least **sensitive** parts of your body! You can test this. Ask a partner to place different numbers of fingers on your back.
Try to guess the number of fingers.
Skin can sense pain, pressure (something touching it), heat and cold.

Scientific words
touch
taste
smell
sight
hearing
eyes
skin
tongue
sensitive

The senses

Touch

Scientific word
organ

Think like a scientist!

The skin is the largest **organ** of the body. It is sensitive. The skin sends messages to the brain so that we feel touch, temperature and pain. The skin on some parts of your body is very sensitive. Your fingers are one of the most sensitive areas of your body.

1

Place a mystery object into a sock. Ask a partner to use only their sense of touch to guess what the object is.

You will need...
- single adult-sized socks
- small 'mystery' objects (such as bar of soap, rock, coin, ball, pine cone)

a Copy the table. Use the headings to record how your partner describes the object.

Name	Describing object with hand outside the sock	Guess after feeling the sock	Describing object with hand inside the sock	Guess after feeling inside the sock

Make sure your partner does not see the object before you put it into the sock!

b Swap places and take turns until you and your partner have described all the objects. Fill in the table as you go.

c Was it easier to guess the object from the outside or inside of the sock? Why?

d Which objects were the most difficult to describe from outside the sock? Why?

e Did the sock make it easier or more difficult to describe the object?

f What did the sock do to the sense of touch?

Unit 4 The senses

Touch test

1

Put a glove on each hand.
Now try to open a book or do another activity!
What happens to your sense of touch? Why?
Use these words in your answer.

- touch
- sensitive
- skin

2

You will need...
- pieces of sandpaper (each the same size) with different textures (each labelled with a letter)
- blindfold

Can you put the pieces of sandpaper in order, from roughest to smoothest, while blindfolded? Try this test.

a Put on the blindfold. Use your little finger to feel each piece of sandpaper. Sort the sandpaper from roughest to smoothest. Take off the blindfold and record your results.

b Repeat the test using your index finger (first finger). Record your results.

c This time, repeat the test using your forearm. Record the results.

d Compare your results. What did you find out about the sense of touch in your fingers and forearm?

Fingerprints

Think like a scientist!

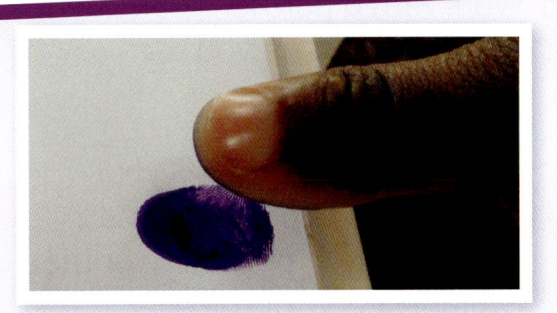

Scientists do not know why humans have **fingerprints**. Every person has a set of fingerprints that are unique (different to everyone else in the world). Even identical twins have different fingerprints. Some scientists think that fingerprints make it easier to grip (hold) things. Others think fingerprints improve the sense of touch.

Types of fingerprints

Most fingerprints have patterns that are arches or loops. Others may have whorls (spirals). Look at these fingerprints.

loop   whorl   arch

1

You will need…
- ink pad
- deflated balloon

Try this fingerprint investigation.

a Press your fingertip in the ink pad. Then press it on the balloon. Leave the ink to dry. Blow up your balloon to see your fingerprint.

b Compare your fingerprint with a partner. What shapes can you see (whorl, loop or arch)?

c Group the others in your class with similar fingerprints by comparing fingerprints.

Scientific word
fingerprints

What shape do you think your fingerprints will be? Now, using a magnifying glass, look closely at your fingertips.

Unit 4 The senses

Sense of sight

Think like a scientist!

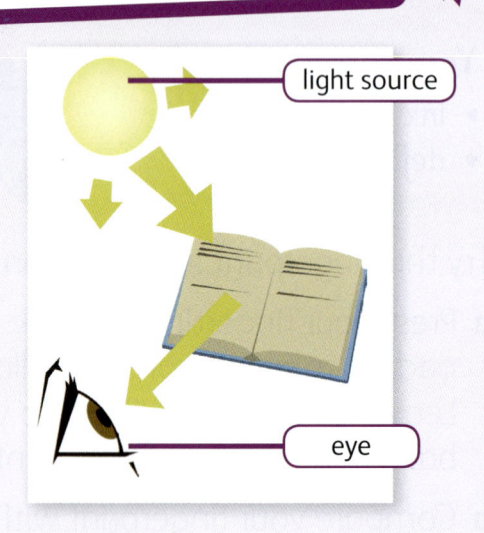

light source

eye

The eyes give you your sense of sight. When your eyes are open, light from the room bounces off objects and enters your eyes. Light enters through the **pupil** – the black hole in the middle of your eye. Light hits **light sensors** at the back of the eye. The light sensors send messages to the brain so that you can see.

The coloured part of your eye is called the **iris**. **Eyelashes** protect the eyes from dust and dirt.

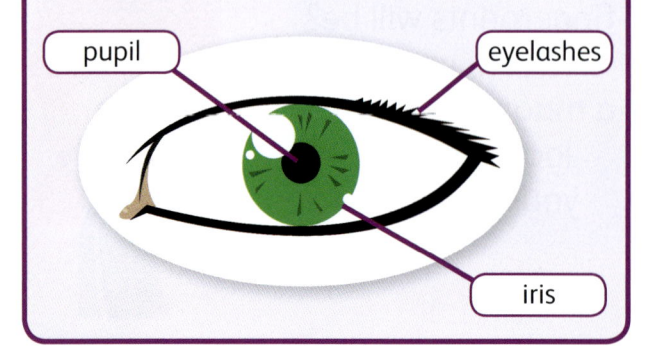

pupil   eyelashes

iris

1

a Work with a partner. Look at each other's eyes. Can you see:
- the iris?
- the pupil? How big is your partner's pupil? (Is it small, half the size of the eye or the biggest part of the eye?)

b Draw a labelled diagram of your partner's eye. Remember to use some of the words in the scientific words box.

Talk partners

Ask your partner to watch you. Close your eyes and count to 50 slowly. Now open your eyes. Ask your partner what happens to your pupils. Swap. Watch your partner doing the same thing. Do some research to find out about the pupils and how they work.

Scientific words
pupil
light sensors
iris
eyelashes

The senses

⟳ Light sensors

Scientific word
nerves

Think like a scientist!

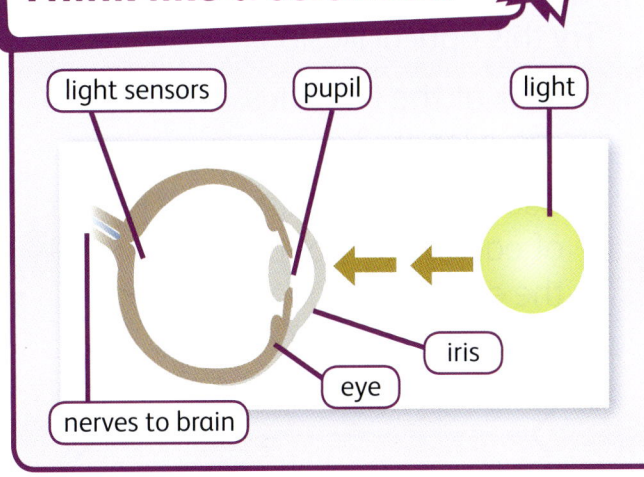

Diagram labels: light sensors, pupil, light, iris, eye, nerves to brain

You now know that light bounces off an object, goes into the eye and hits light sensors. This is the place at the back of the eye where the **nerves** move to the brain. Think of nerves as wires. They lead from your screen (eyes) to your computer (brain). The nerves pass information to the brain so that you can see.

1 Look carefully at the picture of the rabbit and the carrot.

Hold this textbook with your arm held out. Focus on the rabbit's nose. Close your left eye and bring the book closer to your face.
Stop when the carrot disappears. Open both eyes. Is the carrot still there?

a Talk to your partner. Did the carrot really disappear?

b What happened when you did not focus hard on the rabbit's nose?

c Draw some different objects. Can you make one of them disappear? How big must the object that disappears be? Where on the page must the object that disappears be for this trick to work?

The carrot disappears because moving the book closer to your face makes the light bouncing off the carrot hit part of the eye where there are no light sensors. Therefore you cannot see it!

71

Unit 4 The senses

Optical illusions

Think like a scientist!

What do you see – an old lady or a young woman?

Images like this can trick the sense of sight. They are **optical illusions**. Optical means 'sight'. An illusion is something that is not real. Optical illusions work because they trick the senses into sending the brain wrong information.

1

Try this optical illusion.

a Look at the two lines. Are they the same length?

b Use a ruler to measure the length of each line – not the arrows at the ends. How long is each line? Were you correct?

Did you know?

The angle and direction of the arrow heads above trick the light sensors in the eyes. This makes you think that one line is longer!

Challenge yourself!

There are many optical illusions. Do some research to find more. You could use the internet. Then try them out on your class.

Scientific word
optical illusion

The senses

Your nose

Think like a scientist!

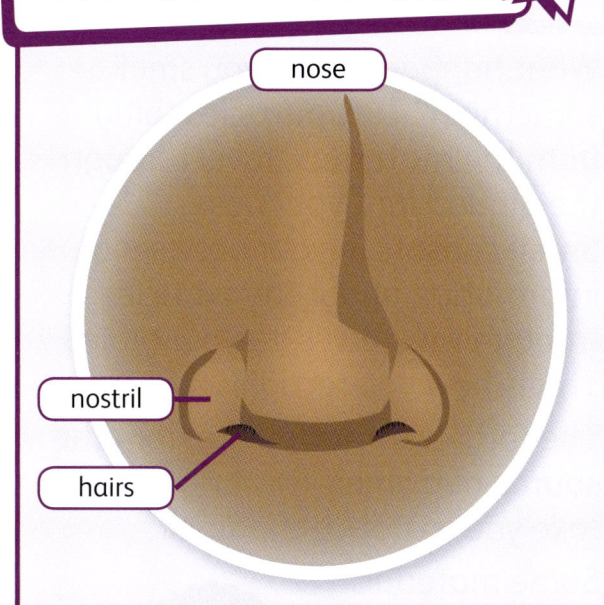

nose
nostril
hairs

The nose gives you your sense of smell. The nose does many jobs:

- **Air** moves in through your nose to your **lungs** (organs in your chest) to help you breathe.
- Tiny hairs called nose hairs are in your **nostrils** to trap dust, so that it does not go into your lungs.
- Your nose warms the air you breathe in before it goes to your lungs.
- Your nose makes **mucus** (snotty stuff) to keep your nose moist. The sticky, slimy mucus also helps to trap dirt and dust.
- Your nose can sense **differences** in smells. Smells can be strong or less strong and pleasant or unpleasant.

1 Use a mirror to look carefully at your nose and draw it. Add labels to your drawing. Use some of the words from the scientific words box. Add anything that is special about your nose to your diagram.

2

lemon   sand
fish   rose   pencil

Look at the pictures.

a Find a way to sort them according to how they smell. You could draw sorting circles.

b Add more examples to your **sorting criteria**.

Did you know?

It is rare (not common) but some people are born with no sense of smell. They smell nothing.

Scientific words

air
lungs
nostrils
mucus
differences
sorting criteria

73

Unit 4 The senses

Smells travel

1

The Class 3 teacher decided to test her learners' sense of smell. She placed some uncooked fish – the source of the smell – on a plate. She hid the plate behind a box in the far corner of the classroom.

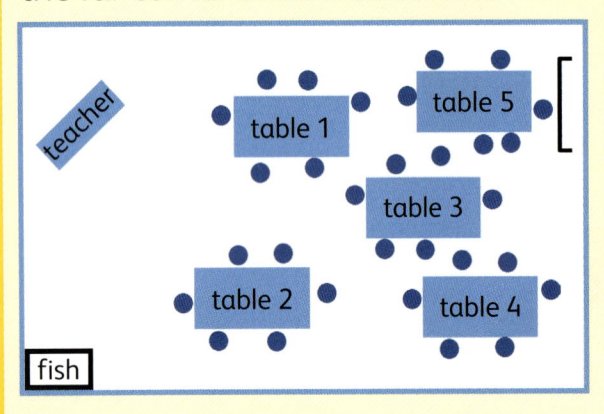

The teacher timed how long it took before the learners at each table started to smell something. She recorded the times in this table.

Table	Time taken to smell (minutes)
2	10
1	20
3	25
4	27
5	35

a How long did it take table 5 to smell the fish? Why?

b Why did table 2 smell the fish before table 1?

Think like a scientist!

What happens when you smell something? Tiny **particles** (bits) from the **materials** travel through the air and into your nose. **Smell sensors** in your nose send information about the particles through the nerves, to your brain. This is how you recognise smells.

The further away you are from the **source** of a smell, the longer it will take you to notice the smell.

Some materials such as perfumes can make many small particles. This is why they have strong smells.

Scientific words
particles
materials
smell sensors
source

c Do you think all the learners at table 2 smelled the fish at the same time? Why?

d What might happen if one learner had a blocked nose. Why?

The senses

Smelling investigation

Think like a scientist!

Some things do not smell until someone cuts, rubs or grinds them. This releases the particles that travel through the air to your nose. Have you been near someone who has cut onions? If you have, what do you remember?

1

You will need...
- five small **opaque** plastic pots with lids (punched with a few holes, numbered 1 to 5 with different types of tea)
- bags of the same teas labelled i, ii, iii, iv, v.

Try this smelling investigation:

a Smell the contents of each pot. Describe what it smells like.

b Does it smell like something you have smelled before? Do you like the smell?

c Match each numbered pot to the labelled tea bags. (For example, *1 = iv*)

d Were you able to match the pots of tea with the bags they came from?

Talk partners

Which pot do you and your partner like the smell of most? Which do you like the least?
Do you and your partner agree on the same smells?

Scientific word
opaque

75

Unit 4 The senses

Smell safety

Think like a scientist!

The sense of smell is important. It helps to keep us safe. For example, the smell of fire may warn us of danger. The smell of rotten food stops us from eating it.

Remember, when you smell something, small particles in the air travel straight into your nose. The air and some particles move into your lungs as you breathe. Many smells can be dangerous when we breathe them in. These contain chemicals, which can cause illness.

1 Copy and complete the table. Use it to show which things are safe to smell and which things you should not smell. The first two have been done for you.

flowers   cleaning products   weed killer   perfume   bath oil   glues   baking bread   coffee   permanent marker pen   sweets   car fuel   wall paint   rotten egg

Object	Safe to smell	Not safe to smell	I am not sure
flowers	✓		
cleaning products		✓	

Challenge yourself!

Research any of the objects that you are not sure about in Activity 1. Are they safe to smell?

Be careful!

Never smell glue. Always check with an adult if you are unsure of a material before you smell it.

The senses

Taste

Think like a scientist!

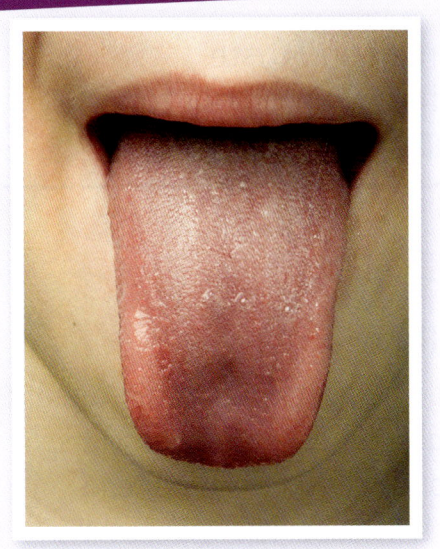

The sense of taste is connected to the tongue and the brain. Your tongue is covered in **taste buds**. Taste buds can identify five tastes: **sweet**, **sour**, **bitter**, **umami (savoury)** and **salty**. The taste buds send messages to the brain to help us to identify different tastes.

Scientists have found out that smell and colour can affect sensors what we taste.

When you chew food, the smell is also carried up your nose to the smell sensors. This helps the brain to identify what the taste is.

When you hold your nose or close your eyes you have less sense of taste.

1

You will need...
- small plastic cups filled with different flavours of juices (such as orange, lemon, lime, mango, guava, pineapple, cherry, blackcurrant, peach, apple)
- blindfold

Try a taste investigation with a partner.

a Take turns to taste each drink with a blindfold on. While tasting, hold your nose. Try to name the flavour of the drink while your partner records it.

b Next, remove the blindfold. Taste each drink while holding your nose (use clean cups). Record your results.

c Finally, taste the drinks as you would normally, and record your results.

d Which drinks were the most difficult to recognise without sight or smell?

e What are your conclusions? Which sense made the most difference to how well you could taste?

Scientific words
taste buds
sweet
sour
bitter
umami (savoury)
salty

Unit 4 The senses

Tasting flavours

Think like a scientist!

Scientific word
saliva

It is the chemicals in food that our senses can smell and taste. When we taste things, the chemicals mix with the **saliva** on our tongues. Saliva is the wet liquid you can feel in your mouth.

1

Try a test to find out if a dry or wet tongue affects the taste.

You will need...
- variety of sweet, sour, bitter, umami and salty foods (such as biscuits, potato snacks, sweets, banana slices, lime slices, dark chocolate, bread, tomatoes, rapini)
- cup of water
- kitchen towel
- stopwatch

a Carefully dry your tongue using a clean kitchen towel. Put a small piece of food on your tongue. What does it taste like – sweet, sour, bitter, umami, salty?

b How much time does it take before you can taste anything? Use the stopwatch to find out.

c Try all the different foods. Dry your tongue before tasting each new food. Copy and complete the table to record your results.

Food	Type of taste: sweet, sour, salty, bitter, umami	Time taken to taste on dry tongue	Time taken to taste on wet tongue
bread			
biscuit			

d After testing all the foods, have a drink of water. Taste the foods again. This time, do not dry your tongue each time.

e What are your conclusions? Does a dry or a wet tongue affect taste?

The senses

Does colour affect taste?

1

You will need...
- jelly beans (one of each colour on a paper plate)
- blindfold

If we can see the colour of a food, do we recognise the flavour? Does the sense of sight affect taste? Work with a partner to try this test and find out.

a Taste each colour of jelly bean without wearing a blindfold. Try to identify each flavour. Copy the table below to record your guess for each flavour.

b Put on the blindfold. Your partner will give you jelly beans to taste (without telling you the colour!). Your partner will write down your guess each time.

c Your teacher will tell you the correct flavours. Add these to your table.

	My guess		
Jelly bean colour	Flavour without a blindfold	Flavour wearing a blindfolded	Correct flavour
red			
green			
pink			
yellow			
white			
black			

d Which colours did you identify correctly – with and without the blindfold?

e Which colours did you identify incorrectly? Why do you think this is?

f Was it easier to identify the flavour with or without the blindfold? Why?

g Which colour of jelly bean was the most difficult to identify? Why?

h When your blindfold was on, what senses did you use to identify the flavour?

i Think about when you knew the colours. How did this affect the taste of the jelly beans? Write your conclusion to the test. Remember to explain why.

Unit 4 The senses

Flavour test

1

Milo wanted to find out if the learners in Class 3 could identify different flavours of snacks without reading the packaging. He put five flavours on different-coloured sugar paper. The flavours he used were:

- cheese and onion
- salted
- tomato
- cheese
- mint

The learners tasted each snack. They named each flavour according to their taste buds. Milo recorded their answers in this table.

	Flavours guessed				
Flavour	cheese and onion	salted	tomato	cheese	mint
red	14	2	1	3	0
yellow	0	5	5	5	5
green	0	2	17	1	0
blue	0	2	2	16	0
black	2	5	2	1	10

(Paper colour)

a Why did most learners guess the flavour on the red paper correctly?

b What flavour did most learners think was on the green paper? Were they right? Why?

c Why did most learners guess the flavour on the blue paper correctly? Which senses other than taste would have helped them to guess?

d What flavour did most learners think was on the black paper? Why do you think some learners made an incorrect guess for this flavour?

e Milo noticed that yellow paper did not have a clear winning flavour. Why do you think this is? Think about the senses learners used to make the guess.

Challenge yourself!

Do you think that the colour of the paper affected some guesses? Explain why.

The senses

Identifying flavours

1

Can you identify (name correctly) different flavours of potato snacks without seeing the packaging? Work with a partner to try a taste test.

You will need...
- four flavours of potato snacks in clear plastic bags, labelled A, B, C and D

a Taste a potato snack from each bag. Taste it and decide on the flavour. Record your answers in a table like this.

Bag	Flavour
A	
B	
C	
D	

b Your teacher will tell you the correct flavour in each bag. Did you identify the flavours correctly?

c Were any flavours difficult for you to identify? Why?

d Which flavour did you find easiest to name correctly? Why?

e Write a conclusion about what made the flavours easier to identify. Was it the smell or a strong taste?

f Did any of the colours or the appearance (what it looks like) help with this test? Which other senses (apart from taste) did you use to identify each flavour? Explain how these other senses helped you.

Which of your senses helped you the most in this test?

Challenge yourself!

Do some research to find out about flavoured potato snacks. Have any scientific tests been done? Which is the most popular flavour of potato snacks in your country?

Unit 4 The senses

The sense of hearing

Think like a scientist!

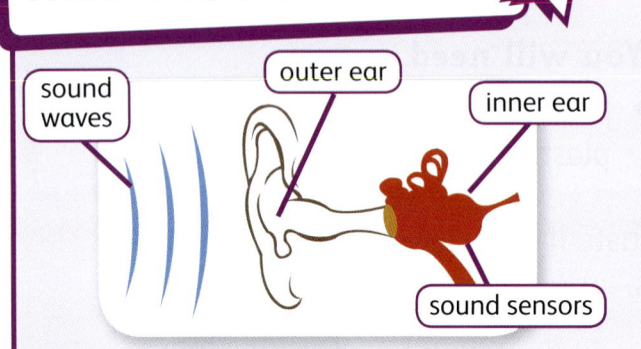

sound waves — outer ear — inner ear — sound sensors

We use our ears to funnel (transport) **sound waves** into our **inner ears**. Sound waves are the way sound travels. We have **sound sensors** – small hairs – in our inner ears. Sound sensors help to send information about the sound waves to your brain. Sound sensors (the small hairs) do not get replaced. This is why many people cannot hear well as they get older – they suffer from hearing loss.

Look after your hearing

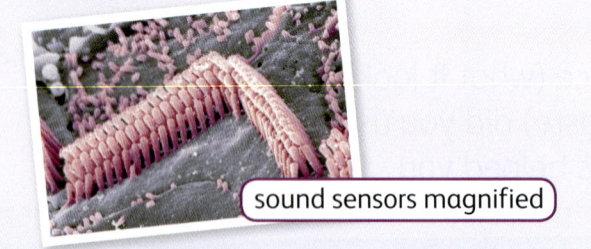

sound sensors magnified

- Protect your ears against hearing loss. Stay away from very loud noises. Use earplugs.
- Children's ears are more sensitive to noise than adults' ears. Sounds are louder because they travel through a smaller space in the outer ear.

1

Keep very quiet. Your teacher will time you for two minutes. Listen to the sounds you can hear in your classroom.

a Now make a list of the sounds you heard. Did you hear birds? Breathing? A clock ticking? Noise from other classrooms? Anything else?

b Sort the sounds you heard into loud, soft, high, low. Were there any sounds that signal danger?

Talk partners

Compare your list with a partner. Did you both hear the same sounds? Who heard more sounds?

Which sounds would be different if you went outside? Do this and compare your lists.

Scientific words

sound waves
inner ears
sound sensors

82

The senses

Hearing sound sources

1

Play a sound game.

a Close your eyes and stand in a space. Ask your partner to walk one metre away from you in a different direction and whisper your name. Point to where you think your partner is. Were you correct?

b Swap and whisper your partner's name.

Scientific words
source of sound

2

Sami and Hal did a test to see how far away from different sources of sound they could hear. The results are in the tables.

Sami – inside the school hall

Source of sound	1 m	5 m	10 m	15 m	20 m
Drum	✓	✓	✓	✓	✗
Maracas	✓	✓	✓	✗	✗
Whisper	✓	✗	✗	✗	✗

Hal – outside

Source of sound	1 m	5 m	10 m	15 m	20 m
Drum	✓	✓	✓	✗	✗
Maracas	✓	✓	✗	✗	✗
Whisper	✓	✗	✗	✗	✗

The object making a sound is called the **source of sound**.

Sami was inside the school hall for his hearing test. Hal was outside.

a Which source of sound could the boys hear further away, inside and outside? Why?

b Was there a difference between hearing sounds inside and outside? Why?

c Do you think their test was fair? Give a reason for your answer.

d Do you think all children hear the same? How might this affect the results?

Unit 4 The senses

Making an ear trumpet

Think like a scientist!

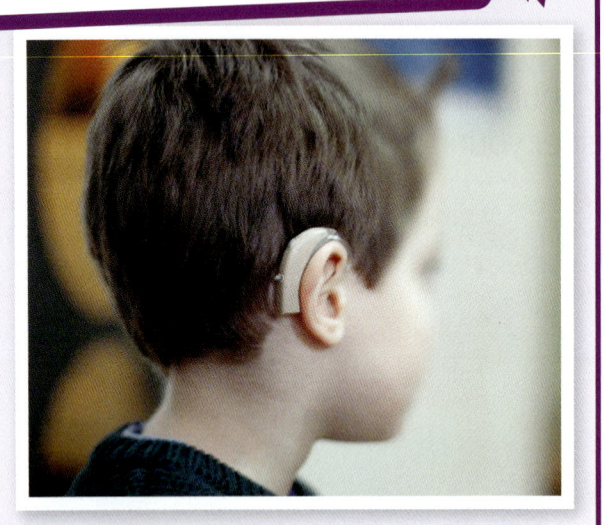

Sometimes hearing is reduced. This means that people cannot hear sounds easily. They may have to wear **hearing aids** to **amplify** (make louder) sounds so that they can hear.

Before hearing aids were invented, people used **ear trumpets** to amplify sounds if they could not hear well.

An ear trumpet is bigger than the ear. So, many more sound waves are directed to the ear – towards the sound sensors. Ear trumpets work very well for hearing soft sounds.

ear trumpet

1

You will need...
- A3 size sugar paper (construction paper)
- sticky tape
- music player and CD

Make an ear trumpet.

a Roll the sugar paper so that one end is as small as possible. The other end must be as big as possible – in the shape of an ice cream cone. Use sticky tape on the edges to keep the cone in shape.

b Place the 'hearing trumpet' with the smallest end to your ear (gently). Do not push the trumpet into your ear!

c Now listen to some music – with your ear trumpet and without the ear trumpet. Does using the trumpet help to make the sound louder? Draw a diagram with labels to explain why. Use the words in the scientific words box.

Be careful

Do not listen to very loud sounds. They will damage your hearing.

Scientific words

hearing aids
amplify
ear trumpets

84

The senses

What have you learnt about the human senses?

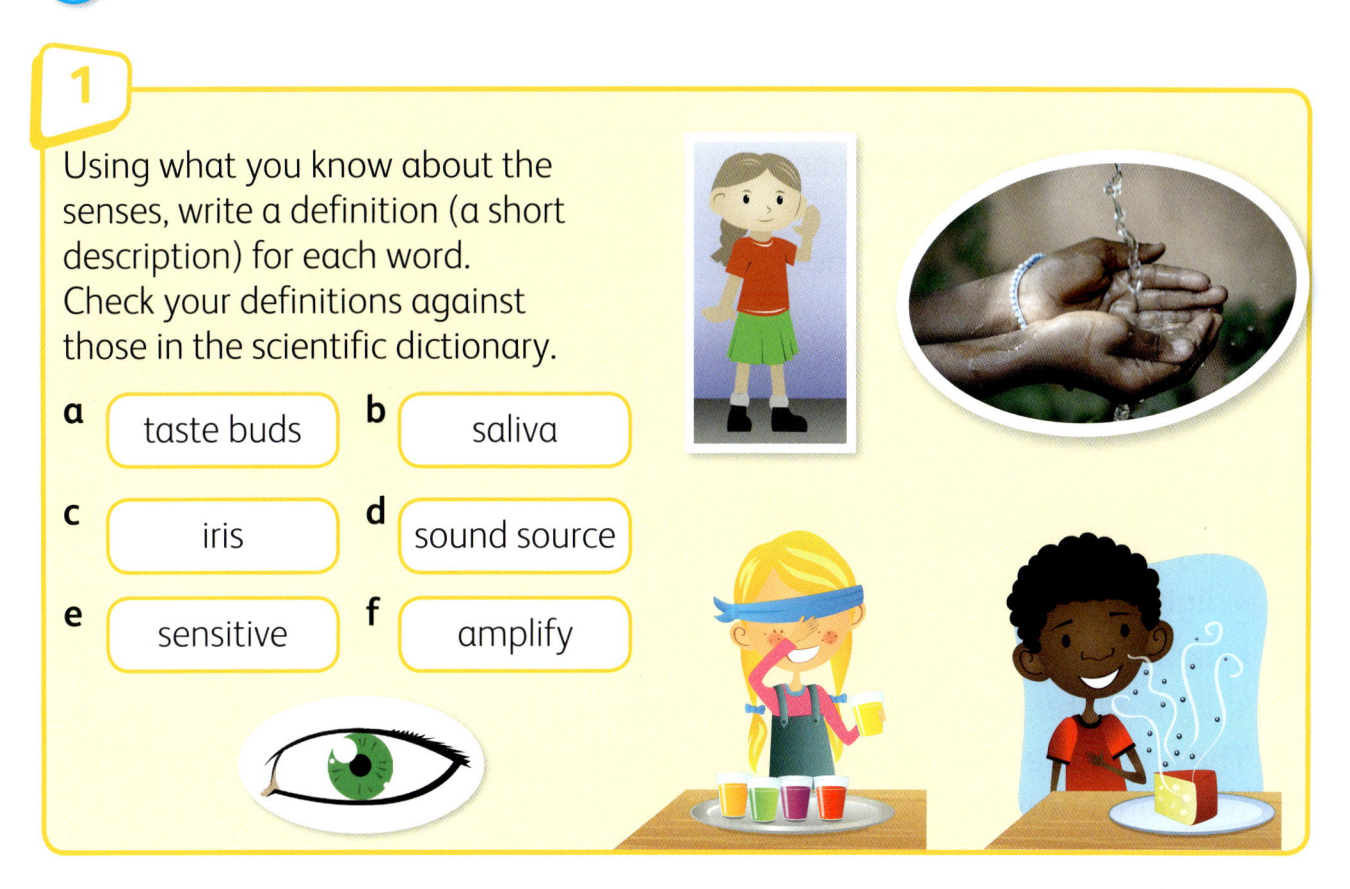

1

Using what you know about the senses, write a definition (a short description) for each word. Check your definitions against those in the scientific dictionary.

a taste buds
b saliva
c iris
d sound source
e sensitive
f amplify

What can you remember?

You have been learning about the human senses. Can you:
- name the five senses?
- name which sense helps us to feel temperature and pain?
- explain how the sense of sight, smell and taste are linked?
- name the largest organ of the body and the sense it is linked to?
- describe an optical illusion?
- explain why an ear trumpet helps us to hear soft sounds?
- name some things that affect your ability to smell?
- explain why it might be dangerous not to be able to smell?
- explain what happens to your sense of hearing the further away you are from a sound?

Practice test 1: Biology

1. Look at this picture of a water lily.
   a What parts of the plant can you see?
   b Where are the plant's roots and stem?
   c What is the job of the roots and stem? (5)

2. Jasmine, Sonia and Tsige investigated what plants need to grow.
   They put plants in pots in different conditions:
   - light, water and heat
   - light, no water and heat
   - light, water and cold.

   They measured the plants at the end of the week. They recorded how tall the plants had grown. Then they created a bar chart of their results.

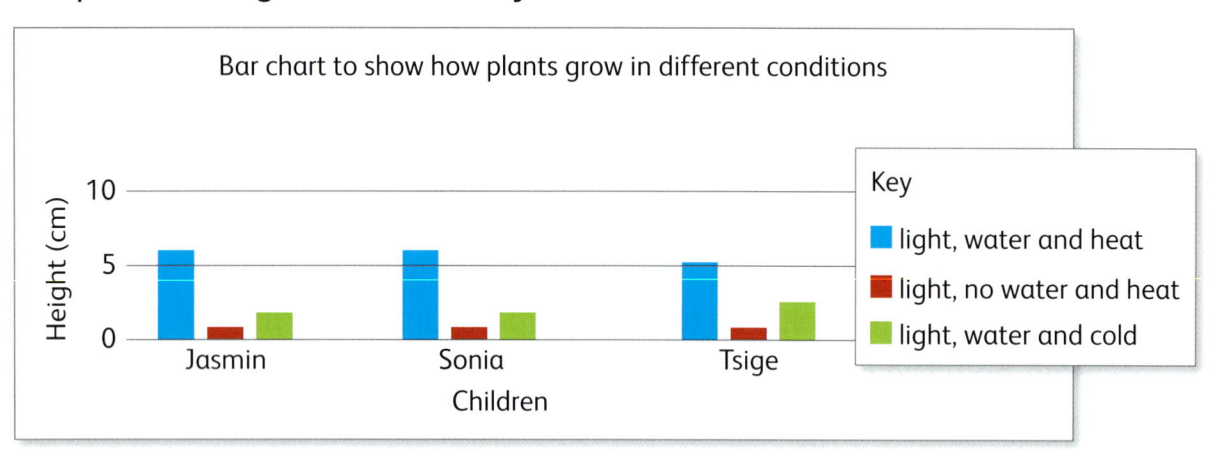

   Bar chart to show how plants grow in different conditions

   Key
   - light, water and heat
   - light, no water and heat
   - light, water and cold

   a In which conditions did the tallest plant grow?
   b In which conditions did the shortest plant grow?
   c Does the temperature make a difference? Explain your answer.
   d What test did they not try?
   e If they had tried this test what do you predict would happen? (5)

3 Look at these objects.

shell | ball of string | stone | cat | person | plant | brick

a Name four life processes that humans and other animals have in common. (4)
b Now sort the objects into living and not living. (2)
c Describe the differences between the objects in the living group. Use some of the life processes. (2)

4 Tumi sorted some pictures of living things using the table below:

	two legs	four legs	six legs	lays eggs	wings
human	✓				
cat		✓			
bird	✓			✓	✓
fish				✓	
snake				✓	
butterfly			✓	✓	✓
frog		✓		✓	

a Then Tumi sorted the living things into two groups. Which features did Tumi use to classify these animals? (1)

bird, fish, snake, butterfly

human, cat

b Tumi also classified them in another way. What property has Tumi now used to sort the animals? (1)

frog, cat

bird, fish, snake, butterfly, human

Practice test 1: Biology

5 Ajay wanted to stay healthy. He found out that some things made his heart beat more often. Look at his table.

Activity	Effect on the heartbeat
watching TV	♥
swimming	♥♥♥
walking	♥♥
reading a book	♥

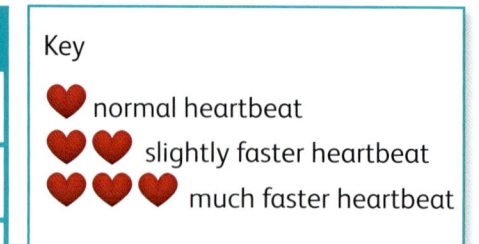

Key
♥ normal heartbeat
♥♥ slightly faster heartbeat
♥♥♥ much faster heartbeat

a Which activity made his heart beat the most?
b Which activity made his heart beat least?
c Name another exercise that Ajay could try that would make his heart beat fast.
d Name one other thing that is important for keeping you healthy (other than exercise). (4)

6 Look at this meal.
a What food group is missing from this meal?
b Which foods in this meal can damage your health if you eat them too often? Why?
c What would make this meal healthier? Change some foods to balance the meal. (5)

88

7 Look at these pictures.

(i) (ii) (iii)

   a Which learner is showing the less healthy lifestyle choice? Why?

   b Explain which two activities are important to keep you healthy. Why? (2)

8 Copy and complete this table by matching the sense organs to the senses in the table. Write an explanation to show how each sense helps us to know about the world.

eyes   ears   skin   nose   tongue

Sense	How it helps us to know about the world
sight	
smell	
taste	
hearing	
touch	

(5)

9 Answer these questions.

   a Imagine that you have a cold and a blocked nose. Which other sense is affected?

   b Which parts of the body can we use for our sense of touch?

   c Why might the skin be called a sense organ?

   d What do you have on your tongue to help you taste different foods? (4)

Total marks: 40

Unit 5 Material properties

What do you know about materials?

Think like a scientist!

Look at the different objects around your classroom – glass, wood, metal, plastic. They have one thing in common (the same). They are all **materials**. All things are made of materials. Even you! Sometimes we call the clothes we wear materials. But scientists call these materials **fabrics**. All materials have different **properties**. A property is what a material can do (how it behaves), looks and feels like. For example, if a material bends, it is **flexible**. If a material lets light pass through it, it is **transparent**. Another material may be **shiny**.

1

water, stone, salt, rubber, sand, wood

Use the pictures to help you think about materials. Create a mind map to describe the properties of each material. What does the material feel like when you touch it? What is its **texture**? What does it look like? What is its appearance? How many scientific words can you use?

a water
b stone
c salt
d rubber
e sand
f wood

Scientific words
materials
fabrics
properties
flexible
transparent
shiny
texture

Talk partners

Share your mind maps from Activity 1 with a partner. What properties did you both use? What information about the properties can you give each other?

Material properties

Sorting objects

1

Choose ten objects from around your classroom.

a Make a table like this one. Write each object and the material it is made from. Remember: some objects may be made from more than one material.

Object	Material(s)
window	glass and wood

b Choose a way to group the objects according to the material they are made from. Draw a diagram to show your results. For example, put objects of the same material into sorting hoops.

c Add a column to your table as shown below. Then add the properties of each material.

Object	Material(s)	Properties
table	wood	hard

d Choose a way to group the materials according to their properties. You could use a flow diagram. Or, think of another way to group the materials. Explain why you have put each group of materials together.

91

Unit 5 Material properties

Describing properties

Think like a scientist!

Ancient Greek scientists thought that all materials belonged to four groups – earth, water, **air** and fire. Scientists today use different groups. They base their groups on properties such as: Can we squash the material? Can we stretch the material?

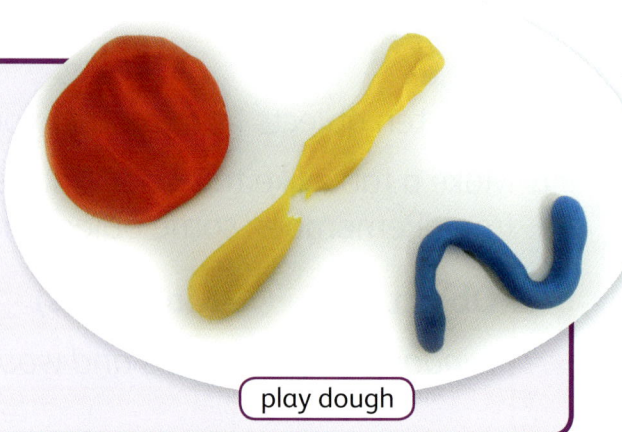

play dough

1

Match these property words with their definitions (meanings). The first one has been done for you.

| hard | **rough** | smooth | **soft** | flexible | **waterproof** | rigid |

a *A material that does not bend or stretch* – rigid
b A material with a surface that is bumpy with ridges
c A material with an even surface without any bumps
d A material that is very firm, solid and not easy to bend or cut
e A material that does not allow water to go through it
f A material that can bend but will not break
g A material that is easy to mould, cut, compress (squash), or fold

Challenge yourself!

Write a definition for each of these properties.

| transparent | **opaque** | **absorbent** | **magnetic** |

Share your definitions with a partner. Do you both agree on the meanings?

Scientific words
air
rough
soft
flexible
waterproof
rigid
opaque
absorbent
magnetic

Material properties

What am I?

1 Match each picture to the correct card. Use what you know about properties of materials to help you.

- bottle of water
- lemon
- coin
- sand
- kitchen towel
- ruler

a What am I?
I am hard.
I am shiny.
I am rigid.
I am man-made.

b What am I?
I can be poured.
I am a liquid.
I am transparent.

c What am I?
I can be piled up.
I am solid.
I am hard.
I am opaque.

d What am I?
I am flexible.
I am absorbent.
I am a solid.

e What am I?
I am rigid.
I am hard.
I am not absorbent.

f What am I?
I am natural.
I can roll.
I have a rough surface.

2 Play this game with a partner. Look around the room and select an object.

- **a** Write three clues. Remember: do not use the names of the objects, only their properties!
- **b** Swap, so that your partner is giving you the clues.
  Play the game again, but use different objects.
- **c** Which objects were the most difficult to guess? Why were they so difficult to guess?

Can you guess this object?
I can be found as a solid, a liquid and a gas.
You could not live without me!
What am I?

93

Unit 5 Material properties

Reflective materials

Think like a scientist!

Shiny objects are usually **reflective**. This means that light is able to bounce, or reflect, off the **surface**. Have you ever seen your reflection in a shiny object such as a metal spoon? **Dull** objects are not shiny. Usually, they are not reflective.

shiny and reflective   dull

1

You will need...
- Objects (such as cork, pencil, mirror, rock, eraser, metal spoon, glass jar, wooden ruler)
- torch, white card, clear plastic cup

object

card – light will reflect here if the object is shiny (reflective)

torch – focused on object

Find out which materials have reflective properties. Set up the investigation in the picture.

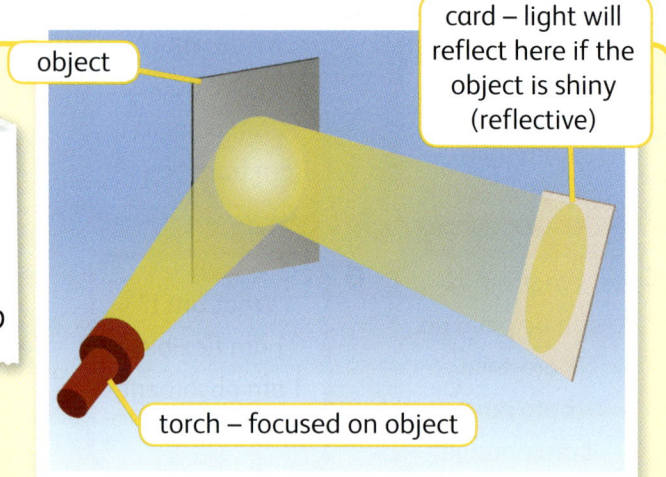

a Discuss how you will carry out this test and make sure it is fair. Think about the position of the object, the torch and the card each time.

b Predict if you think the material will be reflective. Then test each object. Copy this table and record your results.

Object	Material	Dull?	Shiny?	My prediction	Did it reflect light onto the card?
pencil	wood	✓	✗	✗	✗

c Which objects are the most reflective? Which objects are the least reflective? Why? What **evidence** do you have that makes you reach this conclusion?

Scientific words
reflective   surface
dull   evidence

94

Material properties

Sorting materials: Venn diagrams

Think like a scientist!

There are many ways to sort materials.

You can use a simple sorting circle to show materials that share properties.

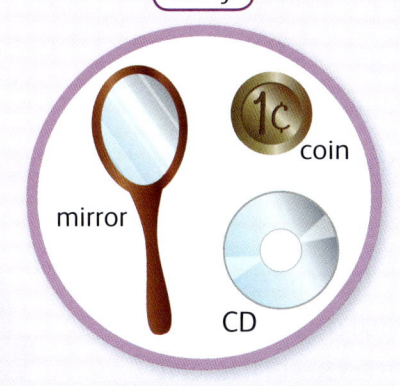

shiny
- mirror
- coin
- CD

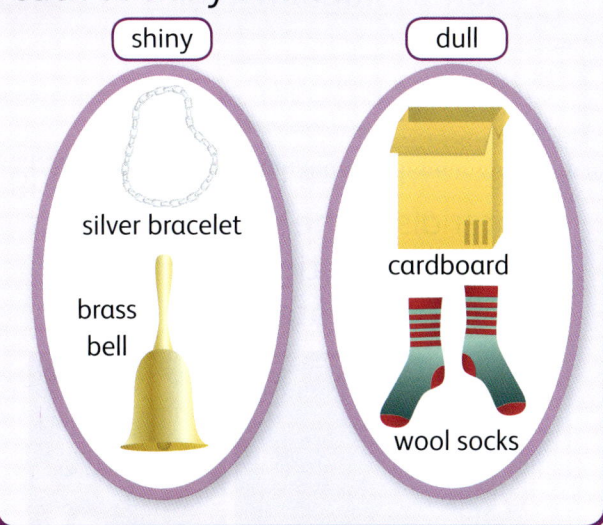

Sometimes you can use a **Venn diagram**. Place objects with both properties in the section where the two circles overlap.

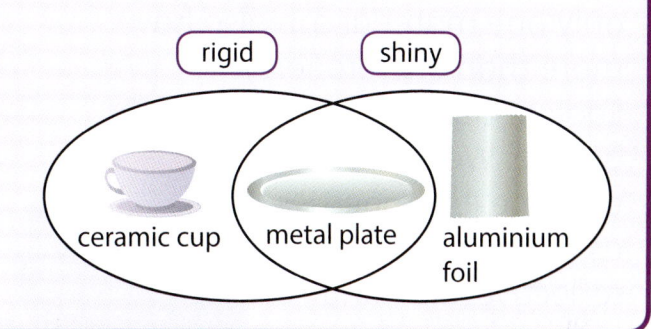

rigid — shiny
- ceramic cup
- metal plate
- aluminium foil

You could use two sorting circles to demonstrate opposite properties such as shiny and dull.

shiny
- silver bracelet
- brass bell

dull
- cardboard
- wool socks

Scientific words
Venn diagram

1

Play a guessing game with a partner. Collect six objects from around the classroom.

a Draw a Venn diagram using three objects. Do not label the sorting circles with the properties yet. Keep this in your head! Make sure you have an object in each section of the diagram.

b Show your diagram to a partner. Your partner must work out the property of each section. Is your partner correct? Now label your diagram to show the properties. Try the game again using different objects.

c Which properties were more difficult to identify? Why?

Unit 5 Material properties

Sorting materials: Carroll diagrams

Think like a scientist!

Some objects are made from more than one material.

Some objects that are made from only one material can also have more than one property. Look at this glass bauble. We can describe its properties as: hard, round, reflective, blue and shiny.

glass bauble

Look at this pumice stone. We can describe its properties as: hard, rough and light.

pumice stone

A **Carroll diagram** is a way to **classify** (sort) objects with more than one **sorting criteria** (sorting methods). The sorting criteria in this table are the object's properties.

	Hard	Not hard
Light	pumice stone	fabric shirt
Not light	wooden table	mattress

Scientific words
Carroll diagram
classify
sorting criteria

1
Choose some of the objects to create your own Carroll diagram. Think about the properties of each. Which objects have properties in common (the same)?

feather   water   cotton wool
rock   modelling clay   coin
balloon   ruler   eraser

The pumice stone is *hard* and *light*. Try to describe the properties of the other objects in your Carroll diagram.

Did you know?

These fruits are the shiniest living materials in the world! Scientists are busy investigating them to invent new materials.

The *Pollia condensata* plant is found in forest areas in Africa. It is also called 'marble berry'.

Material properties

More Carroll diagrams

1

Leon used a Carroll diagram to sort objects according to their properties. One of his sorting criteria was: Are the objects made from shiny material or not?

Look carefully at Leon's Carroll diagram. What is the second sorting criteria that Leon used?

	Shiny	**Not shiny**
_____ ?	new coin compact mirror ring 	button plastic bottle top 
Not ___ ?	metal spoon diamond 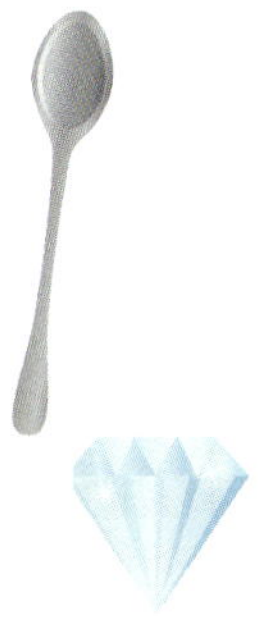	plastic spoon pencil eraser 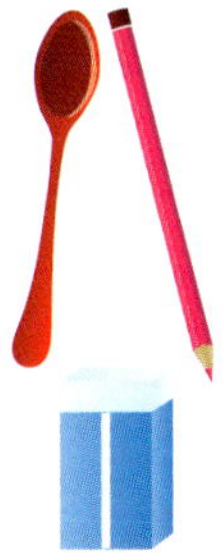

2

Copy and complete this Carroll diagram.

	_____	Not _____
_____		
Not _____		

a First decide on the sorting criteria. Choose two properties and write these on the blank lines in the diagram. Remember to add the opposite for each property! For example: *hard, not hard.*

b Write some objects that will match each property in the diagram.

c Swap your Carroll diagram with a partner to check that it works correctly.

Challenge yourself!

Some properties can never be linked (placed together) in a Carroll diagram. For example, an object cannot be wet and dry at the same time! Look at your Carroll diagram in Activity 2. Which properties can never be linked? Can you think of other properties that can never be linked?

Unit 5 Material properties

Magnetic materials

Think like a scientist!

Some materials are magnetic. This means that they **attract** (pull towards) each other. Magnetic materials are usually made from metal – but not all metals are magnetic. To find out if an object is magnetic you can use a **magnet**. A magnetic object will pull towards and stick to the magnet. Magnets can also attract other magnets, as well as magnetic materials.

magnets attracting metal paperclips

1

You will need...
- magnet
- collection of ten objects from around the classroom

Use the magnet to find out which objects are attracted to it (magnetic) and which are not (**non-magnetic**).

a Predict which objects are magnetic by sorting them into two groups: magnetic and non-magnetic.

b Draw what you have placed in each group. Test each object with a magnet. Were your predictions correct?

c Which materials were attracted to the magnet?

d Which materials were not attracted to the magnet?

Scientific words
attract
magnet   non-magnetic

What do you already know about magnets?

2

Use your knowledge of magnetic materials. Decide if the statements below are True or False. If they are False, try to say why.

a A plastic plate is magnetic.

b A fabric doll is non-magnetic.

c A glass is magnetic.

d An iron nail is magnetic.

e A ceramic (clay) cup is non-magnetic.

Material properties

Sorting magnetic metals

1

You will need...
- magnet
- variety of different coins

Find out if the coins in your country are magnetic.

a Plan an investigation. Think about:
- What will you need to do?
- How will you test your ideas?
- How will you record your results?

b Predict if each coin is magnetic. Then do your investigation and record your results.

c What are your conclusions? Are any of the coins magnetic? What does this mean about the metals they are made from? Write a letter to your teacher to explain your results. Use as many words as you can from the scientific words box.

Scientific words
iron
cobalt
nickel
gold
aluminium
copper

Think like a scientist!

Only some metals are magnetic. These are **iron**, **cobalt** and **nickel**. Coins are usually made of a mixture of metals. If coins contain some magnetic metal, they will be attracted to a magnet. Most other metals such as **gold**, **aluminium** and **copper** are non-magnetic. But, if they are mixed with a magnetic metal, they can become magnetic. If you see that a copper coin is attracted to a magnet, then it must contain some other magnetic metal such as iron or nickel.

These coins are attracted to the magnet.

The coins in the picture contain a mixture of magnetic and non-magnetic metals, so they are attracted to the magnet.

Unit 5 Material properties

Absorbent materials

1

a Sort these objects under these headings:
Absorbent, Not absorbent.

- towel
- raincoat
- cotton wool
- school pullover
- metal coin
- plastic ruler

Think like a scientist!

An absorbent material can take in and hold onto liquid. For example, a sponge absorbs water, so we say it is absorbent.

2

You will need...
- kitchen towels (five sheets)
- food dye (red, blue and yellow)
- water
- five clear plastic cups

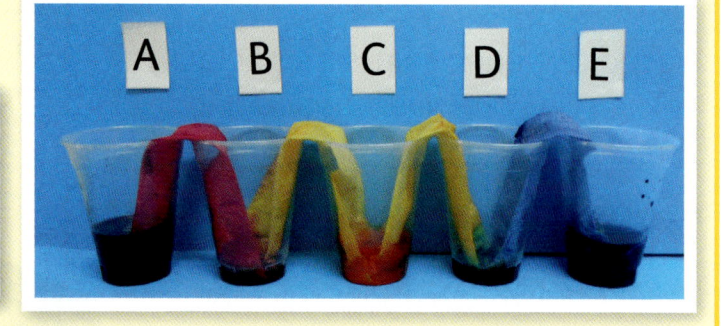

Anouska and Sienna saw this picture in a science book. They wanted to see if they could repeat the investigation in the classroom. This is what they did.

- They placed: red food dye and water in cup A, yellow food dye and water in cup C, blue food dye and water in cup E, no water or dye in cups B and D.
- They lined up the cups from A to E. Look at the picture. Then they folded five sheets of kitchen towel. They put one end of each sheet into the cups.
- They left the cups overnight.

a Try this activity. Were your results the same as in the picture?

b Draw a diagram and explain what is happening to the water and dye. Why is this happening? Use the scientific words that you know.

c Why is it important to leave cups B and D empty?

Material properties

Absorbency investigation

Remember, if a kitchen towel is absorbent it should hold the water and not let it out. Do all kitchen towels absorb the same amount of water? Do the investigation in Activity 1 to find out.

kitchen towel

1

You will need...
- different types of kitchen towels
- hand lens • microscope • ruler
- food colouring • water • clear plastic pots
- metal tray • measuring beaker • pipette

a Plan an investigation. Think about:
- What equipment will you need?
- What will you do to test the different types of kitchen towels?
- How will you make it a fair test?
- How will you measure and record the results?

b Predict which type of kitchen towel will be best and why.

c Do your test and record the results.

d Which type of kitchen towel was best? Or were they the same? Present your results. What are your conclusions and why?

e Look at the kitchen towels under a hand lens or microscope. Is there anything about the materials that makes some kitchen towels more absorbent? Share your ideas.

f Create a poster about which type of kitchen towel people should buy.

Challenge yourself!
Do the investigation again. Use a different material. Find out if it absorbs liquid in the same way.

Did you know?
Upsalite

By accident, Swedish scientists left on some equipment in their laboratory over a weekend. Without knowing it, they invented the 'impossible material' Upsalite. It is the most absorbent material in the world today! Sometimes, making a mistake is good!

101

Unit 5 Material properties

Waterproof materials

Think like a scientist!

Waterproof materials do not let water pass through them. They **repel** liquid (let liquid run off them). A waterproof coat will keep you dry when it rains.

waterproof raincoat

1

Look at and think about these objects. Sort them into waterproof materials and not waterproof materials.

- socks
- boots
- T-shirt
- paper
- sponge
- umbrella
- glass cup
- kitchen towel
- rubber gloves

Hint: Think about the type of material and its properties.

2

How many waterproof things can you find in your classroom?

a Collect materials or objects from around the classroom.

b Make a simple table like this. Separate the waterproof objects from those that are not waterproof.

Waterproof	Not waterproof

c Are the objects that are not waterproof always absorbent? Remember that absorbency means taking up water and holding on to it.

Talk partners

Scientific word
repel

How many waterproof objects can you name that you have at home? What room in your house has the most waterproof materials?

Material properties

Waterproof test

1

Zeta discovered a hole in her tent. She decided to fix it with a waterproof patch. She was not sure which material to use.

You will need...
- patches (small squares) of different materials (such as rubber, fabric, plastic-coated fabric, plastic, wool, felt, leather)
- cup of water
- teaspoon (or pipette)

a Plan an investigation to test each patch to help Zeta. Think about:
  - What will you do?
  - How you will keep the test fair?
  - How you will record the results? You could use a table like this:

Material	My prediction	Waterproof	Not waterproof
paper		✗	✓

b Predict whether a material is waterproof or not. Then do your test and record your results.

c Present your results to a partner. What are your conclusions?
   Were your predictions correct?
   Which material would be best for Zeta to use as a patch? Why?

d Put the materials in order from least waterproof to most waterproof.

e Is there anything that all waterproof materials have in common?

Did you know?

The most waterproof material in nature is a butterfly wing. Scientists took slow-motion videos where they saw how water runs off butterfly wings. They found that the tiny ridges (folds) on the surface of the wing made more water run off it.

People drop their mobile phones in water often. This is why companies now use material with ridges to make phones more waterproof. Humans are learning from butterflies!

Unit 5 Material properties

Hard and strong materials

Think like a scientist!

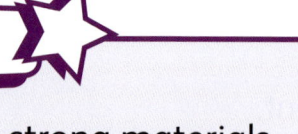

Hard materials are generally strong materials. But, we measure hardness and strength in different ways. Hard materials such as metals do not scratch or dent (mark) easily. Soft materials such as chocolate are easy to scratch and dent. Strong materials do not break easily. A weak material is one that breaks easily.

nail

wax candles

chocolates

stones

1

A hard material is one that cannot be scratched easily. Talk to a partner. Decide how you will find out which object is made from the hardest material using the equipment listed.

a Plan the investigation and decide how you will record your results. Predict which materials are the hardest and say why.

b Carry out the investigation and record your results.

c Which material was the hardest? Put the materials in order, from the softest to the hardest.

d Look around your classroom. Find a material that you think will be:
  • softer than all the materials you have just tested
  • harder than all the materials you have just tested.

You will need...
- range of objects such as rock, chalk, coin, pencil, candle, plastic ruler, ceramic tile, ball of clay
- nail
- hand lens

Did you know?

Diamonds are the hardest material on the planet. The word 'diamond' comes from the Greek word meaning unbreakable. Diamonds are so hard that they can be used to cut and polish other materials.

Material properties

Paper strength

Think like a scientist!

Strong materials are difficult to break or tear. To test how strong something is (its strength), a **force** must be applied. A **weak** material tears easily. In the past, parchment paper was made from reeds and vellum paper from animal skins. Today, paper is made from wood. Not all paper is the same strength.

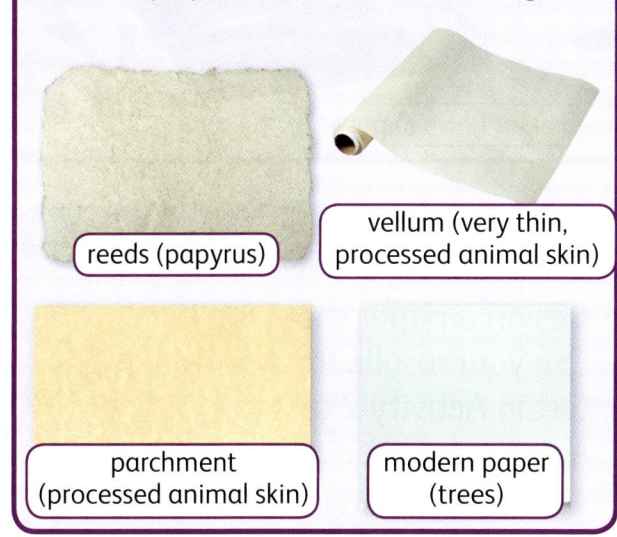

reeds (papyrus)

vellum (very thin, processed animal skin)

parchment (processed animal skin)

modern paper (trees)

Scientific words
force
weak
fibres

1

Collect different types of paper.

a Which type of paper do you think is the strongest? Which is the weakest? Why?

b Tear them. Look at them using a hand lens or microscope. What do you notice? Can you see the **fibres**?

2

You will need...
- strips of different types of paper
- hole punch
- marbles
- yoghurt pot
- paperclip

paper
hole
paperclip
yoghurt pot
marbles

Carry out a test to find the strongest paper.

a Predict which paper will be strongest. Give a reason.

b Cut strips of paper, each the same size. Punch a hole in the middle of each strip, in the same place each time.

c Using a stretched paperclip, make a hook for hanging the yoghurt pot.

d Count the number of marbles each strip will hold in the yoghurt pot before the paper breaks. Record the results.

e Which paper was strongest? Order the strips from strongest to weakest.

Unit 5 Material properties

Design a paper shopping bag

Think like a scientist!

Think back to your investigation in Activity 1 on page 105. You saw that paper is made from interlocking (connecting) plant fibres that are woven together. It is harder to tear if you try to tear it horizontally (across the fibres). It is easier to tear vertically (along the fibres).

Leaving paper in the sun also changes the fibres. It makes them smaller, and this affects the strength.

magnified plant fibres in paper

1

Leave a newspaper in the sun for two days. Then test its strength against a new newspaper.

a Tear each paper vertically (top to bottom) and horizontally (left to right). Do they feel the same?

b Which paper is stronger? How has leaving the paper in the sun affected the strength?

c Use a hand lens or microscope to look at the torn edges of both papers. Can you see the fibres? What do you notice about the fibres of the paper that you left in the sun?

Challenge yourself!

Design a paper shopping bag. Use your results from the weight test in Activity 2 on page 105 and Activity 1 on this page. Think about:
- Which paper was the strongest in the weight test?
- Which paper had many fibres, so should be stronger?
- How did the sun affect the paper?
- Which types of paper are weak? Why should you not use them to make a shopping bag?

Draw and label a design for your paper shopping bag. Remember to explain your choice of paper and why you chose it.

Material properties

Ajay's new clothes

Think like a scientist!

Scientific word
durable

Look around the classroom. Can you spot any objects made from fabric? Some fabrics must be **durable** (hard-wearing and strong). For example, people walk on carpets. This can weaken (wear out) the fabric or material from which it is made. Therefore, carpets need to be durable.

1

Ajay wanted to buy some new clothes made from strong fabrics. Try this investigation to discover which fabrics are durable and which are not.

You will need...
- round pebble
- fabric squares (such as cotton, wool, felt)
- a hard floor

Wrap one fabric square around the pebble. Rub the pebble on a hard floor ten times. Check if the fabric has a hole. Copy and complete the table to record your results.

a Predict which fabrics are the most durable.

Fabric	Hole	No hole
cotton		✓

b Test each fabric and record your results.

c What are your conclusions? Which fabric is the most durable? Is it suitable (right) for making clothes?

d Which fabric is the least durable? Why?

e Which fabrics would be best for Ajay's new clothes? Draw an annotated diagram (with labels and information) of Ajay in new clothes made from these fabrics. Include information about the fabrics you have chosen and why.

Is a durable fabric always suitable for making clothes?

107

Unit 5 Material properties

Materials for a purpose

Think like a scientist!

glass windows with wooden frames

Materials have different properties. We choose them for different purposes (**functions**). For example, a glass window and one made of cardboard do not have the same properties. A cardboard window will not let in light and will become soggy when it rains!

1

a Record all the different materials you can find in a table like this:

Object	Material	Use
ruler	plastic	measuring/ drawing lines

b Look at your table and choose a way to sort the materials into groups. For example, you could draw the objects in sorting hoops according to what they are made from.

c Put the objects that are made of more than one material into a separate group.

d Talk to a partner about the materials in your groups. Why is it that some objects are always made from one material? Why can other objects be made from more than one material?

Scientific word
functions

Challenge yourself!

Find five objects that are made from more than one material. Identify the materials and their properties. Say why they were chosen for making the object. Some examples have been given to help you get started. Try to list as many properties as you can.

Object	Materials	Properties and purpose
desk top	plastic	hard, solid, not absorbent, easy to clean
desk legs	metal	strong, solid, not flexible so holds up desk

Material properties

Suitable and unsuitable materials

Think like a scientist!

Materials are usually chosen because of their properties. For example, glass is usually chosen for making window panes. Glass is suitable because it lets light through. It is strong and does not let the wind or rain in. It would be very strange to make a window pane out of chocolate! Chocolate would be a very unsuitable material because it is opaque (not see-through) and would melt and break easily!

1

This table shows different materials and properties.

Materials		Properties	
wood	stone	strong	waterproof
glass	concrete	hard	long-lasting
metal	chocolate	shiny	easy to shape
plastic	leather	absorbent	fragile
fabrics	ceramic	flexible	opaque
brick	paper	rigid	transparent

teapot   waste paper bin   drinking cup   toy

a Choose one object and two materials from the table above. One material used to make them must be suitable. The other must be made from unsuitable material. Create a table to show why each material is suitable and unsuitable. Use the property words above to help you.

b Choose another object and add it to your table in **a**.

109

Unit 5 Material properties

New materials

Think like a scientist!

Before a scientist develops a new material, she or he needs to think about what the new material will be used for. All materials have properties. Most materials have more than one property. It is the mixture of properties that make materials useful for some objects. Here are some examples of new materials:

- 'Potatopak' is made from potato starch. It is used to make trays, plates, bowls, cups and containers.
- 'Fastskin' is used to make swimsuits. It increases a swimmer's speed through water by being extra smooth.
- 'Smart fabrics' are used to make sports clothing and outdoor wear. These fabrics keep you cool when you are hot. They also keep you warm when you are cold!

potatopak

fastskin

smart fabrics

1

Design a new material with special properties. You do not have to make it, so you can be as imaginative as you like!

a Draw and label your material. Answer these questions about the material:
- What are its properties? (Use the words on page 109 for ideas.)
- Why is this new material so special?
- What will it be used for?
- Will it be a mixture of different materials, in order to combine certain properties?

b Create a poster to advertise your new material. Explain what it can do and why it is excellent. What items can customers buy, made from this new material?

110

Material properties

Properties of sports shoes

Think like a scientist!

Sports shoes are made from a variety of materials that are chosen for their properties. For example, they make the people wearing them run faster and feel more comfortable.

Some sports shoes are made from **polyurethane** – a very strong and hard-wearing material. This means that runners can run long distances with one pair.

'bootie' for water sports

Some, as shown, are the shape of feet and made from leather. Leather is strong and gives the feeling of wearing no shoes. However, there is little cushioning under the foot, so it is not comfortable on some surfaces.

1

Look at the materials and properties below. Select six materials. Decide why or why not each one would or would not be suitable for making sports shoes.

Materials		Properties	
wood	rock	strong	waterproof
glass	concrete	hard	long-lasting
metal	chocolate	shiny	easy to shape
plastic	leather	absorbent	fragile
fabrics	ceramic	flexible	opaque
brick	paper	rigid	transparent

Scientific words
polyurethane
biodegradable
recyclable

biodegradable sports shoe

Did you know?

Some sports shoes have seeds built into them! They are made from **biodegradable** materials. When they are worn out, they are **recyclable** and can be planted in the ground. Flowers will grow from the old shoe!

111

Unit 5 Material properties

Designing sports shoes

Talk partners

Talk to a partner. Discuss what the most amazing sports shoes would be able to do, have or look like.

What would be useful about sports shoes with built-in lights?

1

Imagine that you are a designer. Create a pair of sports shoes that everyone will want to buy.

a What special properties will the shoes have? Make them unique (one of a kind) or make them so that they are very different.

b Think about everything you know about materials. What materials will you choose for making the shoes? Look at the table below to get some ideas.

Material	Properties
kevlar	10 × stronger than leather
kangaroo leather	springy for extra comfort and stretch
polyurethane	strength of metal, stretchiness of rubber
canvas	thin and flexible
gel soles	cushions the feet

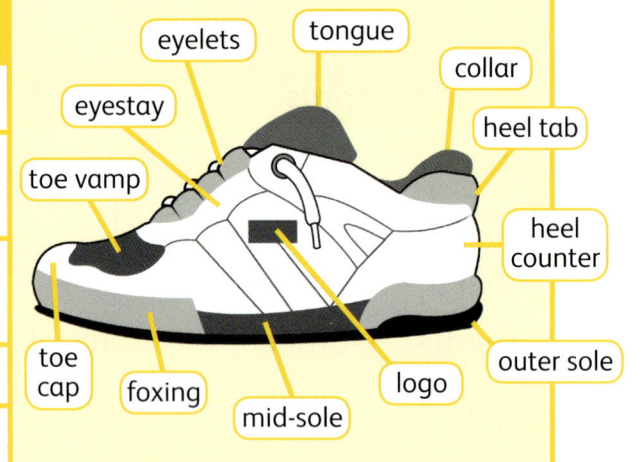

c Draw a design of one shoe. Use the example diagram to help you to design the different parts of the shoe. Will you use the same material for each part?

d Describe the materials you will use. Why will you use them? Add labels to show the special properties of the materials you have chosen for each part of the sports shoe.

e Give your shoes a name that highlights their special properties. An example could be, *Springfast*, for a sports shoe made from kangaroo leather.

Material properties

What have you learnt about material properties?

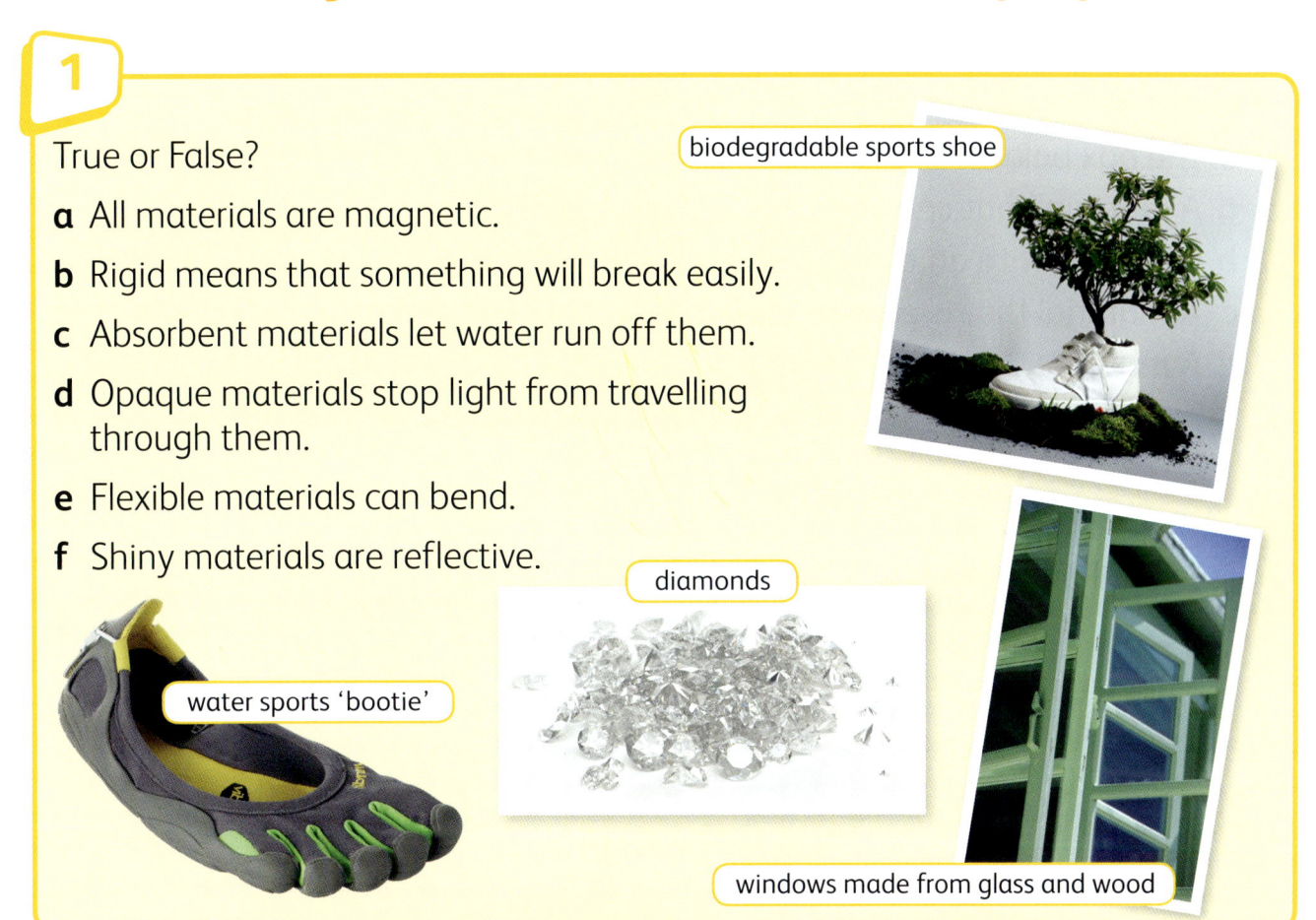

1

True or False?

a All materials are magnetic.
b Rigid means that something will break easily.
c Absorbent materials let water run off them.
d Opaque materials stop light from travelling through them.
e Flexible materials can bend.
f Shiny materials are reflective.

biodegradable sports shoe

water sports 'bootie'

diamonds

windows made from glass and wood

What can you remember?

You have been learning about material properties. Can you:
- name four common materials that are found in school?
- explain what a property is?
- choose an object in the classroom and list its properties?
- use a Venn diagram to sort a selection of objects according to their properties?
- explain what a Carroll diagram is?
- name a magnetic metal?
- name a non-magnetic metal?
- explain, using its properties, why a material is suitable for an object?

Practice test 2: Chemistry

1 Match the descriptions of these definitions with their meanings in the box below.
  a A material that can bend but will not break
  b Materials with an even surface without any bumps
  c A material that is easy to mould, cut, compress or fold
  d A material that does not bend or stretch

  smooth   flexible   rigid   soft   (4)

2 Look at these objects.

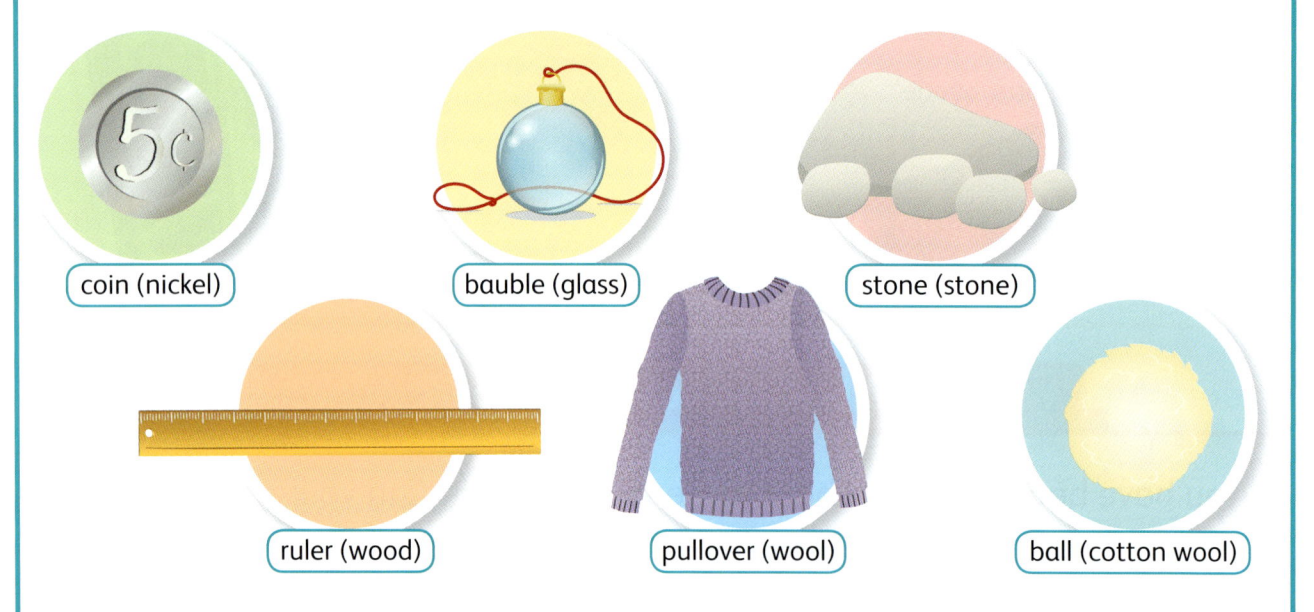

  coin (nickel)   bauble (glass)   stone (stone)
  ruler (wood)   pullover (wool)   ball (cotton wool)

  a Sort the objects under the headings: Hard, Soft.
  b Which object is made from a transparent material?
  c What is the difference between man-made and naturally-occurring materials?
  d Which objects are made from man-made materials?
  e List three properties of the wooden ruler.
  f Which object may be magnetic? Why?   (6)

3 Answer the questions below about these objects.

iron nail | wooden spoon | fabric cleaning cloth | plastic drinking cup | paper kitchen towel

   a Sort the objects under the headings: Flexible, Rigid.
   b What does 'absorbent' mean?
   c Which objects may be absorbent?
   d What does 'waterproof' mean?
   e Which object is waterproof?
   f Which object will be attracted to a magnet? Why? (6)

4 Materials with flexible properties can change shape. Look at these objects.

stone | metal spoon | play dough | brick | book | elastic band

   a Which objects are flexible?
   b If you used your hands to change the shape of the objects, which objects would not be flexible? (4)

5 Imagine that you will make each object below. Choose a material from the box to make each object. Use the material properties to explain your choice. Use each material only once.

glass | fleece | fabric | plastic fabric | metal | wood

   a blanket   b raincoat
   c saucepan   d table
   e jug
   (5)

Total marks: 25

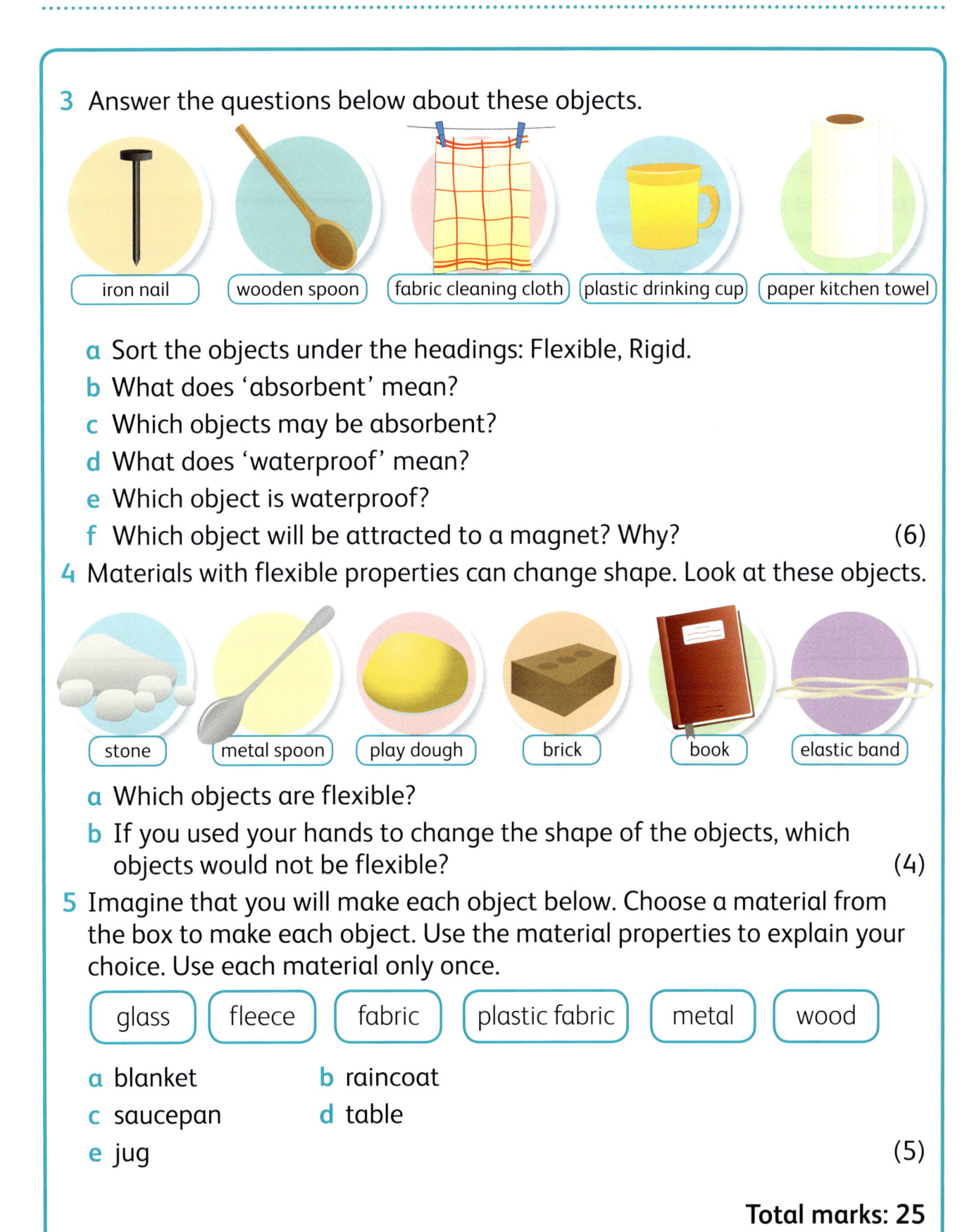

115

Unit 6 Forces and motion

What is a force?

Think like a scientist!

Objects do not move by themselves. They need a physical **force** to make them move. A force is something that we cannot see. But we can see the **effect** of a force on an object.

This boy is using physical force to jump on the trampoline.

A force is either a **push** or a **pull**. For a push or a pull to happen there must be two objects.

When Lucas jumps on his trampoline he pushes down. The **flexible** material of the trampoline pushes back on his feet. The effect is that he bounces in the **air**. The material and Lucas are both needed for the effect of the forces that make Lucas bounce and the trampoline move.

1 Look at these pictures closely. Think about what is happening. Then answer the questions.

What do you already know about forces?

a Where are the forces at work in the pictures?
b Is each force a push or a pull?

Scientific words
force
effect
push
pull
flexible
air

116

Forces and motion

Pushes and pulls

Think like a scientist!

A push is when you use a physical force to move something away.

A pull is when you use a physical force to move, or bring, something towards you.

1 Look at these pictures.

a Sort them into 'push' and 'pull'.
b What pushes and pulls have you used today?
c Look around your classroom. Then make a list and draw diagrams to show if each is a push or a pull. Where do you need to use a push or a pull?

What have you pushed and pulled today?

2 Sadia and Nakita are going canoeing. They must wear these special clothes. Sort the items into push or pull to show which force they must use when putting them on.

117

Unit 6 Forces and motion

Weight, mass and force

Scientific words
weight
mass

Think like a scientist!

The **weight** of an object is the force pulling down on it. The heavier the object, the more force pulling it down, making it more difficult to move. Mass is different to weight. **Mass** is the amount of material in an object. We measure mass in grams (g) and kilograms (kg).

1

Talk about these action pictures with your partner.

A writing
B shutting a drawer
C moving a chair
D using an eraser

a Decide if the pictures are examples of a push or a pull.
b Do you and your partner agree?
c Try out any actions you disagree on.

Challenge yourself!

Put these classroom activities in order of how much force is needed to move the object.
1 Opening a classroom door
2 Opening a cupboard door
3 Lifting the teacher's chair
4 Lifting a pencil

2

The vehicles in this picture have broken down.
Which vehicle will need the most people to push it off the road? Explain why.
Use the scientific words in the box and any others that you know.

Forces and motion

Measuring forces

Think like a scientist!

We use a **force meter** to measure forces (such as weight) in **newtons** (written as N). One side of the scale on a force meter measures the force in newtons. The other side of the scale shows the mass in grams or kilograms.

All force meters have springs. The spring stretches when you hang an object on the hook. This is because the object is applying a force. The plastic ring moves to show the measurement of force in newtons (N) and the mass in grams per kilogram (g/kg) of the object on the hook.

- spring
- plastic ring that moves up and down
- scale showing force in newtons (N)
- little nut (to calibrate) must be put back to 0 if it is not there at the start
- hook for objects
- yellow force meter (50 N/5 kg)

1

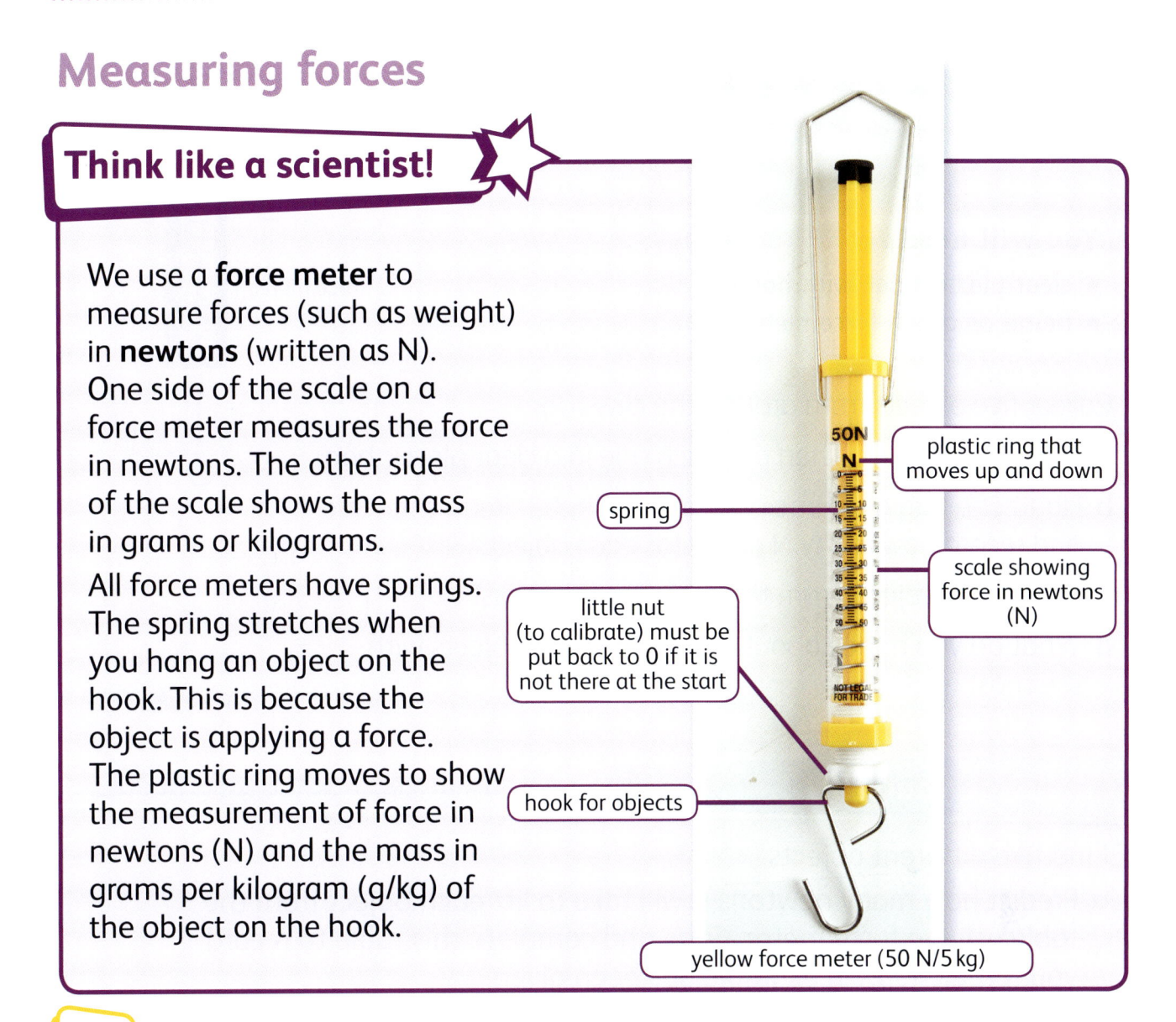

When you hang an object on a force meter, **gravity** pulls it down. Gravity is a pulling force that keeps us on our planet.

a Hook different objects on a force meter. What happens to the spring once the object is attached to the hook?
b What is the force in newtons for each object?
c What is the mass of each object in grams or kilograms?
d Which object has the most N (greatest force)?
e Which object has the least N (least force)?

Scientific words
force meter
newtons
gravity

119

Unit 6 Forces and motion

Practise using a force meter

1

You will need...
- clear plastic bags with handles
- beige or green force meter

force meter

Collect five objects from around the classroom.

a Draw each object. Then put each one in a clear plastic bag.

b Hang one bag at a time on the force meter. Read the scale and record how many N and g for each object.

c Order your objects from the most N to the least N.

d What do you notice about the mass of the objects with the most N?

Challenge yourself!

Find five different objects.

a Predict how many newtons it will take to lift each object from the table using a force meter. Copy and complete this table to record your prediction. An example has been given.

Object	My prediction in N	Actual N	Actual mass in g
book	3 N	2 N	200 g

b Use a force meter to measure how many newtons it takes to lift each object. Record the actual N and the mass in your table.

c Which object took the most force in newtons? Explain your answer (include the word 'mass').

Is 'lifting' a pushing or a pulling force?

Forces and motion

Different force meters

Think like a scientist!

Force meters are made in different colours. The force meter that a scientist chooses to use depends on the mass of the object it can hold. Look at the mass that these force meters can hold.

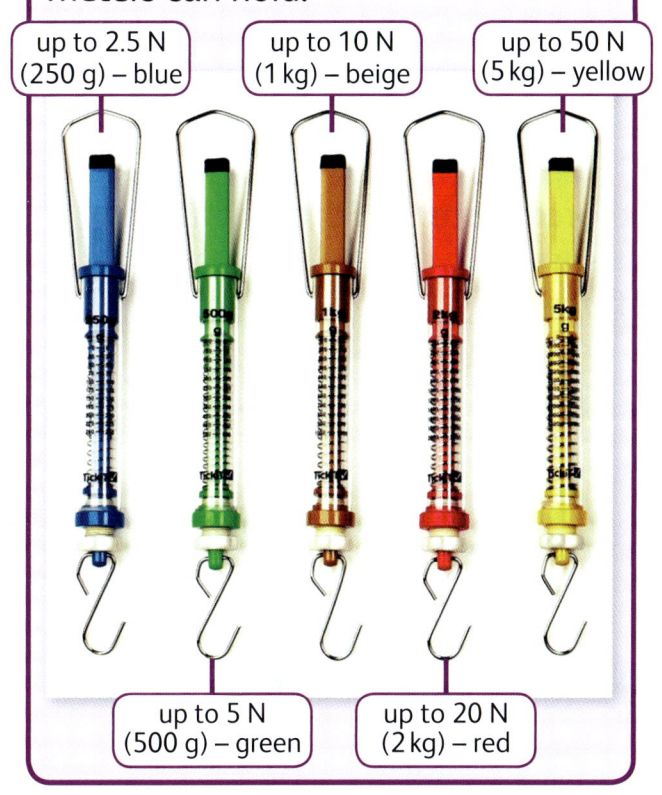

- up to 2.5 N (250 g) – blue
- up to 10 N (1 kg) – beige
- up to 50 N (5 kg) – yellow
- up to 5 N (500 g) – green
- up to 20 N (2 kg) – red

Did you know?

Newtons are named after Sir Isaac Newton, the scientist who discovered gravity. He found out that the bigger the mass of an object, the bigger the force that is needed to move it.

1

Look at these two force meters.

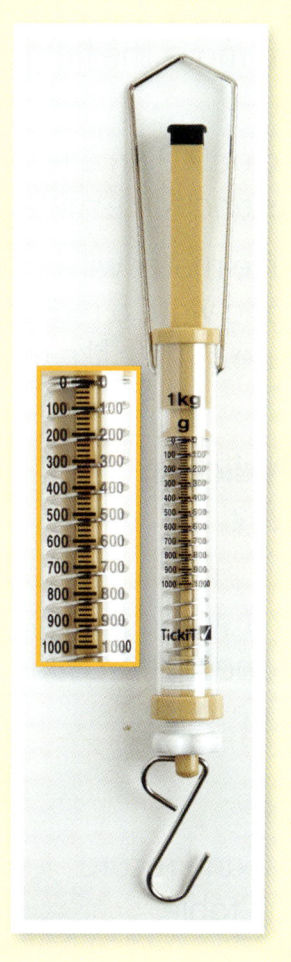

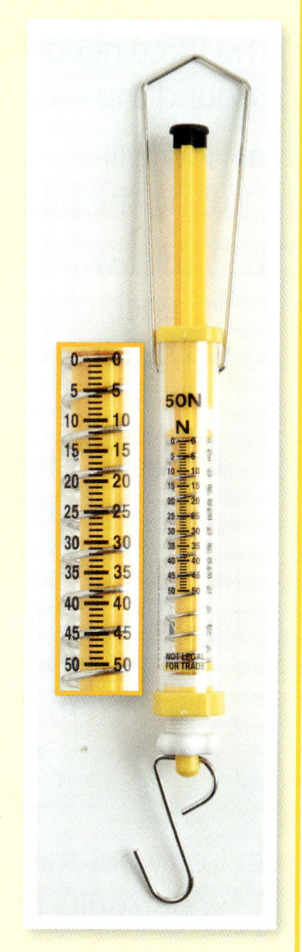

Identify how they are the same and how they are different. Copy and complete this table to record your ideas:

Similarities	Differences
both have springs	the springs are different sizes

121

Unit 6 Forces and motion

Choosing a force meter

1

Which force meter is best for measuring the force needed to move the items around the room?

a How will you find out? Plan a test using the objects and force meters.

b Predict which force meter will be best for each object and write a reason why. You could use a table like this:

You will need...
- selection of force meters (yellow – 5 kg/50 N, red – 2 kg/20 N, beige – 1 kg/10 N, green – 500 g/5 N, blue – 250 g/2.5 N)
- brick
- textbook
- coat
- bag of sugar
- chair
- school bag

Object	My prediction and why	Best force meter for measuring the force	Force measured (N) to move the object
brick	I think it would be best to use the red force meter because....	red	12 N

c Carry out the test and record your results in the table.

d Were your predictions correct? What are your conclusions?

Hint: Think about the weight of the object when choosing a force meter. Is the object heavy or light?

Talk partners

Work in pairs and use a beige (1 kg/10 N) force meter. Give your partner an amount of force to pull using the force meter. With closed eyes, your partner must try to pull that amount. Then, with eyes open, your partner should check to see if the amount of force is correct. Swap places and repeat.

Forces and motion

Making a force meter

1

Make your own force meter by following these instructions:

You will need...
- piece of card 10 cm × 30 cm
- ruler • pencil • string
- hole punch
- split pin (drawing pin)
- paperclip (opened)
- elastic band • plastic cup

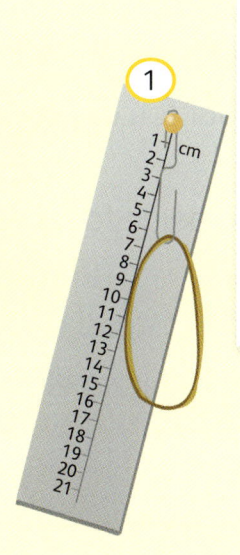

1 Draw a scale down the piece of card using the ruler and mark on the cm. Make a hole with the hole punch on one end of the scale. Insert the split pin. Fasten one end of the paperclip around the split pin.

Hang the elastic band over one loop of the paperclip.

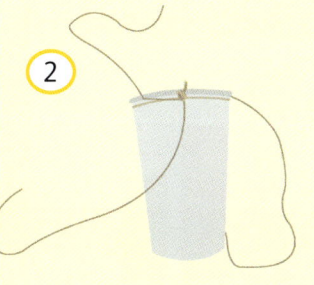

2 Make three holes, equally spaced around the rim of the cup. Insert a piece of string through each hole and tie a knot to fasten the string tight.

3 Tie the three pieces of string through the elastic band, as you can see in the picture.

4 Try out your force meter!

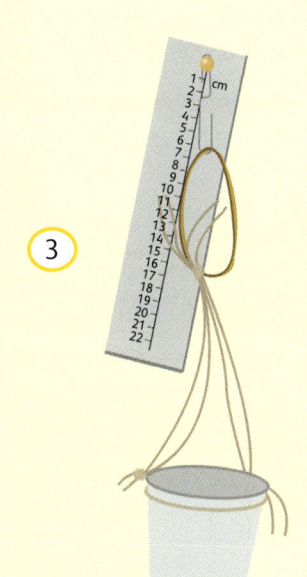

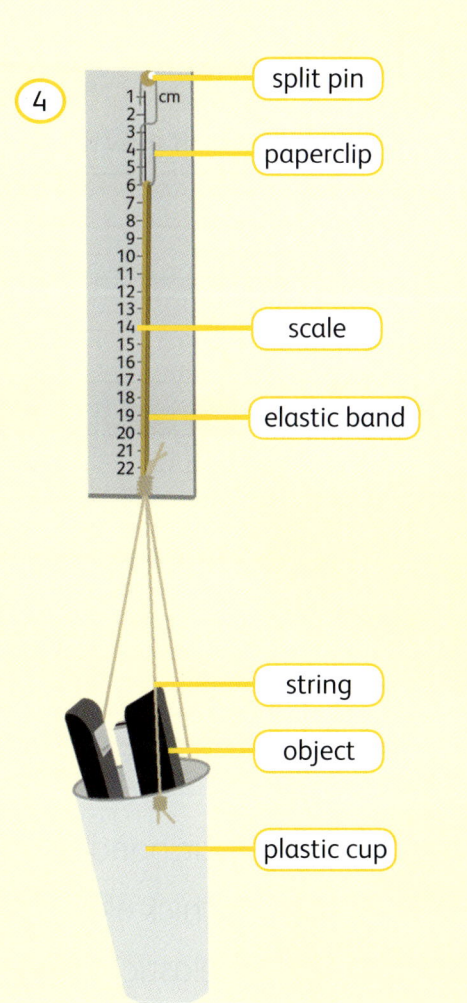

- split pin
- paperclip
- scale
- elastic band
- string
- object
- plastic cup

123

Unit 6 Forces and motion

Evaluate your force meter

Scientific word
bar chart

1 How well does your force meter work?

a Try measuring an object with your force meter and write down the measurements in cm.

b Measure the same object with a beige force meter. Are the measurements the same? If not, why not?

c What does your force meter have instead of a spring?

d What would happen if you used a thicker elastic band? Why?

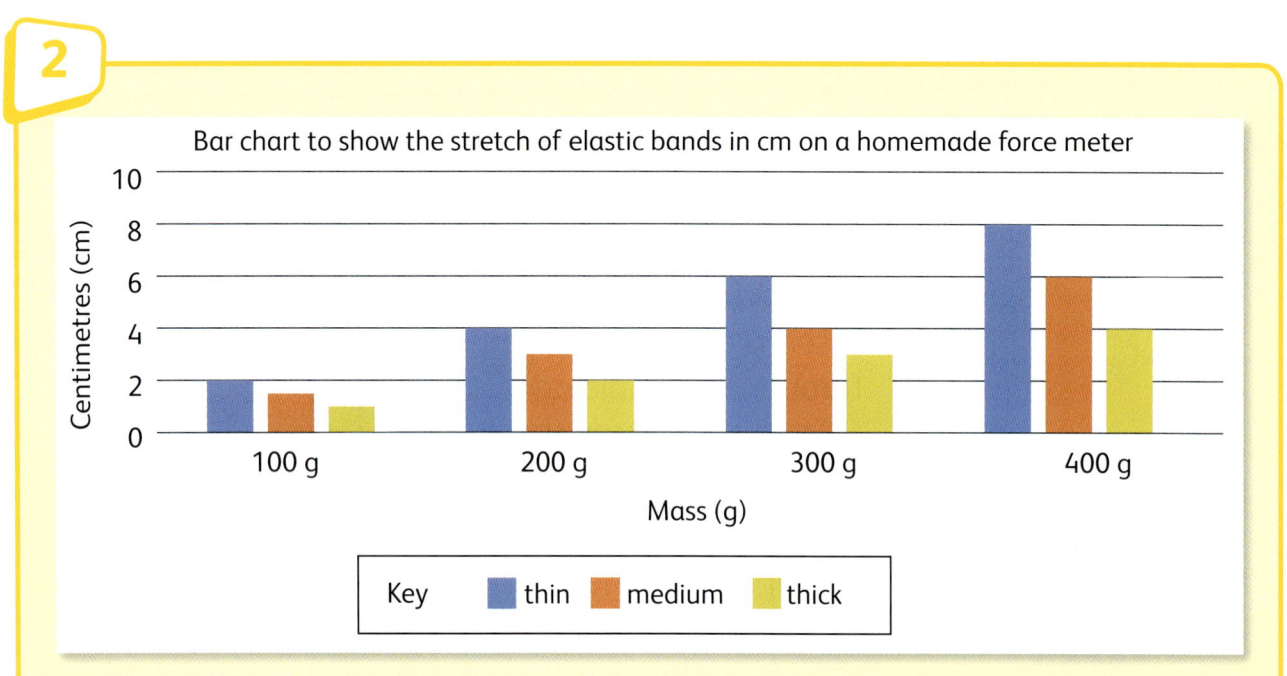

2

Bar chart to show the stretch of elastic bands in cm on a homemade force meter

Key: thin, medium, thick

The **bar chart** shows what happened to the stretch of different elastic bands on a homemade force meter when mass was added. Are these statements True or False?

a The thick elastic band stretched less than the thin elastic band.

b At 200 g, the thick elastic band stretched 5 cm.

c The medium elastic band stretched 4 cm when 300 g was added.

d At more than 300 g, all the elastic bands broke.

Forces and motion

Starting objects moving

Think like a scientist!

When an object moves or changes direction, forces are working. Most forces are invisible, so we show them using arrows. Arrows can show the direction and size of a force. Look at the forces in these pictures.

large → small →

forwards → ← backwards

1

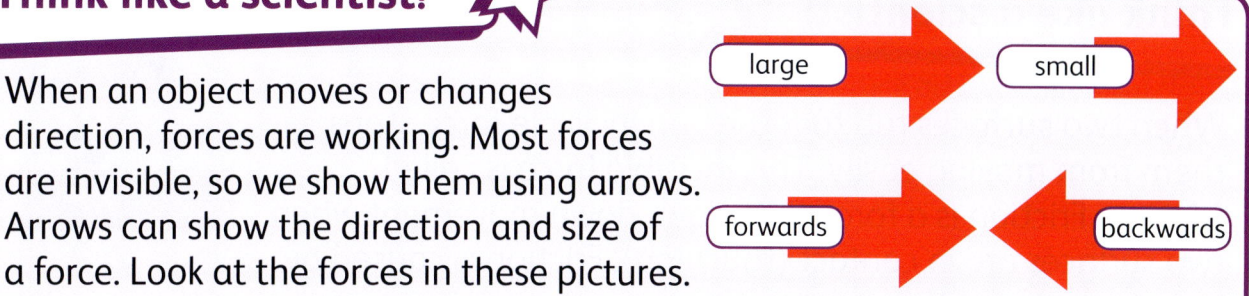

Push a marble with your finger. Try a small push and then a bigger push. Measure the distance the marble travels each time in centimetres.

You will need...
- marbles
- ruler

a What happens to the distance when you increase the force (push)?

b What do you have to do to change the direction of the marble?

c Draw a diagram with arrows to show the size and direction of the force in questions **a** and **b**. Include how far the marble travelled.

d What else might affect how far the marble travels?

Challenge yourself!

Make a blow-football game. Use a cardboard box, straws for goals and a paper ball. To play, start the ball in the middle. Blow it with a straw to move it towards each goal.

a What force makes the ball move?

b What happens to the ball when you increase the force?

c How can you make the ball move slower?

d How can you change the direction of the ball?

e Try the game using a different ball such as a marble. Is there a difference in the force you need, compared with the paper ball? Why? Explain your answer using the words 'mass' and 'force'.

Unit 6 Forces and motion

Stopping objects moving

Think like a scientist!

When two **surfaces** rub together, an invisible force stops them from moving easily. This invisible force is called **friction**. Friction is a force that slows down movement when two surfaces are in contact (touching). Friction is caused by the roughness of the surface. This slows down the movement of the object.

1

a Rub your hands together fast. What do you feel?

You will need...
- olive oil

b Now put a small amount of olive oil onto your hands. Rub them together fast.

c Compare the two rubs. Which was easier? Talk to a partner about the difference between when you rubbed with oil and rubbed without. Use the words 'friction' and 'surface' in your answer.

Scientific words
surfaces
friction

2

You will need...
- smooth board
- wooden block

Look at the picture.
Set up the board and block in the same way.

a Make a prediction. What will happen to the block when one end of the board is lifted slightly? Why?

b Lift one end of the board slightly. What happens to the block? Was your prediction correct?

c How did the surface of the board affect the way the block moved? Draw a picture with labels and the words 'friction' and 'smooth surface' to explain what happened.

d Would you get the same result if you used a rough board? Why?

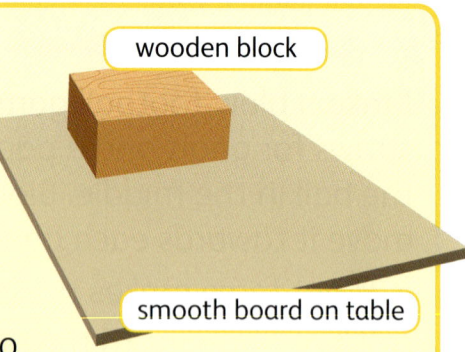

Forces and motion

Surfaces and friction

Think like a scientist!

When things slide easily the surfaces are smooth so there is less friction or we say that the surface has **low friction**. When surfaces are **rough** there is more friction or have a **high friction** so things do not slide as well.

1

You will need...
- smooth piece of wood
- ruler
- empty matchbox
- small rock
- small plastic cube
- cotton wool ball
- ice cube

Find out which objects move the fastest down a slope and why. Put all the objects at the end of the piece of wood. They should all be in the same starting position.

a Slowly tilt the wood until the objects start to move. Record which objects move first.

b Put the objects back in the starting position. Repeat the activity at least three times. Scientists always take more than one reading. This helps them to be more certain of the results. Record how high you had to raise the wood in cm before all the objects began to move.

2

Try Activity 1 again, but use a metal tray instead of the piece of wood.

a What are the similarities and differences in the way the objects move on metal compared to moving on wood?

b Which surface (wood or metal) has the lowest friction (smoothest surface)?

c Why do you think some objects moved before others? Use 'friction' and 'surface' when writing your conclusion.

Scientific words
low friction
rough
high friction

127

Unit 6 Forces and motion

Investigating high and low friction

Think like a scientist!

Friction works between the tyres of a car and the road. This gives grip and stops the car from sliding. Grip is very useful when rain falls on road surfaces. A wet road has low friction (a smooth surface), so is more likely to make a car slide. Different types of cars have different tyres. The thicker the tyres and the more ridges (the rougher the surface), the higher the friction between the tyre and the road surface.

1

Look at these pictures. Do they show high friction or low friction?

a) slipping on a floor
b) soles of hiking shoes
c) coming down a slide
d) plastic grip mat

Talk partners

Talk to your partner about other examples of high friction and low friction that you know. When can friction be helpful? When might friction be a problem?

Did you know?

The surface of a normal car tyre has high friction (is rough). This is helpful, as it stops the car from sliding on the road. However, normal car tyres are not helpful for racing cars that want to go fast! Racing cars tyres have low friction – they have smooth surfaces. There is less friction to slow them down.

a normal car tyre

racing tyre

128

Forces and motion

Changing friction

1

Try this investigation to change the effect of friction on gelatine cubes. Place one cube on the ceramic plate. Try to pick it up with the chopsticks!

You will need...
- gelatine cubes
- chopsticks
- granulated sugar
- paper plate
- ceramic plate
- cooking oil

a Was it easy or difficult to pick up a cube? Why? Try to use the words 'high friction' or 'low friction' in your answer.

b What happens if you put the cube on a paper plate? Was it easier or more difficult? Why?

c Try pouring a little cooking oil over a few cubes on the ceramic plate.
Does this make it easier or more difficult? Why?

d Roll some cubes in granulated sugar. Now try to pick up the cubes from a ceramic plate. Describe the effect of the sugar on the friction between the cube and the chopsticks.

e Was there high friction or low friction on the sugared cubes?

f Was there high friction or low friction on the oiled cubes?

Think about the different surfaces of the ceramic plate, cubes and chopsticks!

Did you know?

Friction can change, depending on the amount of surface that is in contact with (touching) an object. So, if two shoes of different sizes have the same soles, the larger shoe may have higher friction than the smaller shoe. This is because more of the larger shoe is in more contact with the surface to grip it.

129

Unit 6 Forces and motion

Sledges

1

Find out which sledge will move a small toy the greatest distance on a ramp.
Make a ramp by placing two books under a whiteboard.

You will need...
- small toy
- small boxes (such as matchboxes) with different materials stuck on the bottom (base) (such as cotton wool, sandpaper, aluminium foil, bubble wrap)
- books
- smooth surface (such as small whiteboard)
- tape measure
- glue
- ruler

a Look at the different materials on the bottom of each matchbox. Sort the matchboxes into those with a high friction base and those with a low friction base.

b Predict which base will move the toy the greatest distance and the shortest distance in the sledge.
Use the words 'high friction' and 'low friction' in your predictions.

c First test a matchbox sledge with no material on the base. If it slides down, start your test. If it stays at the top of the slope, add another book to make your ramp steeper.

d Record your findings in a table like this:

Type of material	Distance travelled in cm
foil	
sandpaper	

e Were your predictions correct?

f Which sledge travelled the furthest distance? Why? Try to use the word 'friction' in your answer.

g Which sledge travelled the shortest distance? Why?

h How did you make the test fair?

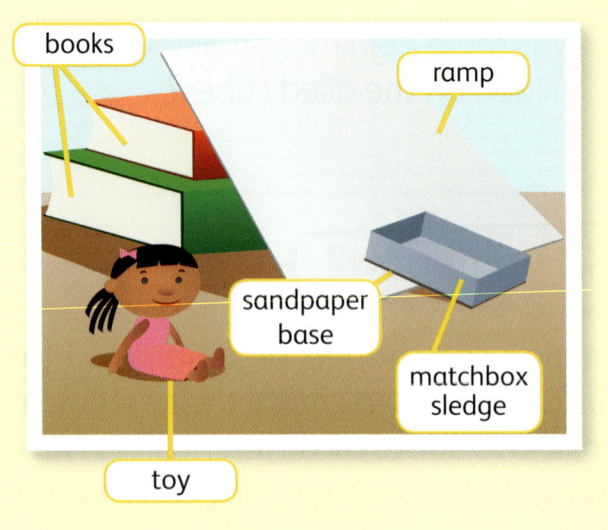

130

Forces and motion

The best surface for a sledge

1

Abimbola and Ebele carried out the toy sledge activity on page 130. They recorded their results in the bar chart below.
They forgot to add the materials they used on their bar chart.

a Help them by matching matchbox sledges 1 to 4 to these materials.

sandpaper   cotton wool   aluminium foil   cardboard

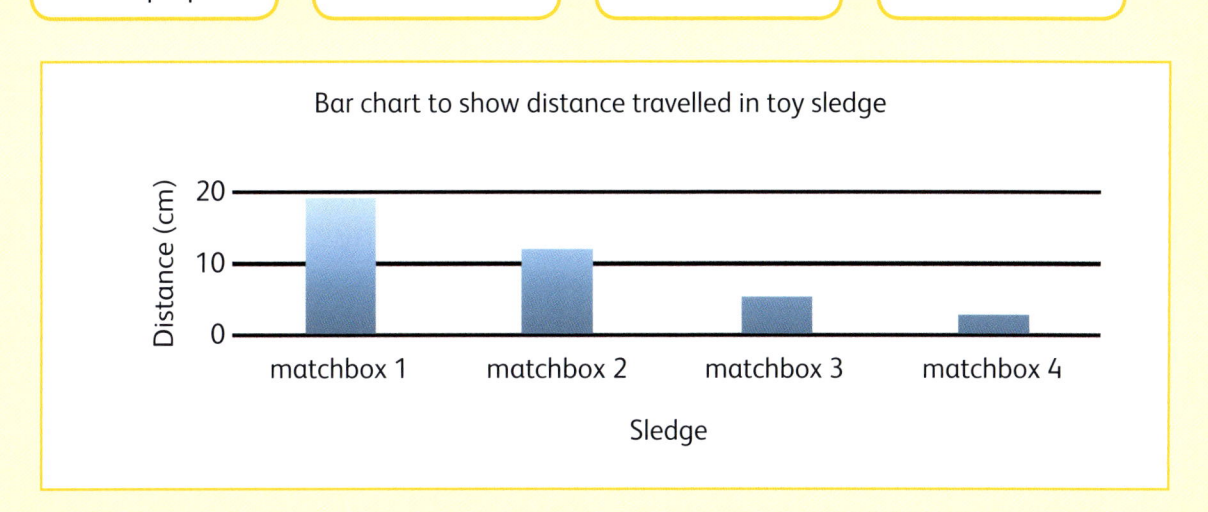

Bar chart to show distance travelled in toy sledge

Distance (cm): matchbox 1 ≈ 20, matchbox 2 ≈ 12, matchbox 3 ≈ 5, matchbox 4 ≈ 3

Sledge

b Which sledge took the toy the furthest distance? Explain why, using the scientific words 'low friction' and 'surface'.

c Which sledge took the toy the shortest distance? Explain why, using the words 'high friction' and 'surface'.

Challenge yourself!

Design a board for sliding over a snowy surface. Which materials would you choose to make the surface of the board? Explain why this material would give the fastest ride. Use what you know about friction and surfaces in your explanation.

Do you want the material to be high friction or low friction?

Unit 6 Forces and motion

Friction of shoes

Scientific word
evidence

Think like a scientist!

Friction can be useful in walking boots, for example. Their rough soles (base of the shoe) provide high friction, giving the shoes a good grip. A good grip is important to prevent people from slipping on smooth surfaces such as ice, shiny surfaces or wet grass.

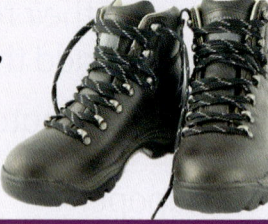

1

You will need...
- range of shoes with different soles
- string
- plastic bag
- force meter
- ramp
- ruler

Plan a test to find out which shoes have the most friction. Decide on one thing you will change and one thing you will measure.

Things that you could change:
- type of shoe
- surface on which you test them.

Things you could measure:
- amount of force (newtons) to move the shoe on each surface
- the height of a slope before the shoe moves.

For example, you could decide to change the type of shoe and measure the height of a slope before the shoe moves.

a Draw and label a diagram to explain what you will do.

b How will you make sure it is a fair test?

c Predict which shoe will have the most friction and why.

d Carry out your test. Record your results in a table that shows what you are changing and what you are measuring, for example:

Change	Measure
type of shoe	*height of slope before shoe moves (cm)*
school shoes	
flip-flops	

e Put your results into a bar chart.

f Which shoe has the most friction and what **evidence** shows this?

Challenge yourself!

Try putting your results into a bar chart.

132

Forces and motion

Mass, weight and friction

Think like a scientist!

The mass and weight of an object affects the amount of friction when moving it. Also, a heavier box has a greater force, so will push down more on the floor. This gives the surface higher friction when you try to move the box than a lighter box. The heavier box will be harder to move than a lighter box.

1

Try this test to see how heavier objects have more force than lighter objects.

You will need...
- play dough
- matchbox
- small heavy weights (coins or marbles)

a Roll some play dough flat on your desk. Place an empty matchbox on top of it, then lift it. Did it mark the play dough?

b Now place something heavy inside the matchbox. Place that on the play dough and then lift it. Did it mark the play dough now?

c Compare the two. Which left the biggest mark and why? Use the words 'force', 'mass' and 'weight' in your answer.

d Does more contact between the object and the play dough make friction higher or lower?

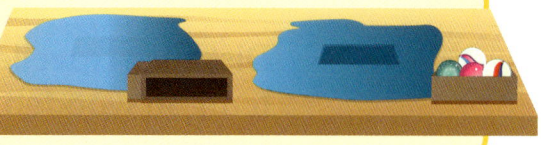

Talk partners

Talk to your partner about what happened in Activity 1. Think of examples in everyday life when it becomes more difficult to move something when it gets heavier.

Unit 6 Forces and motion

Reducing friction with wheels

Think like a scientist!

Wheels reduce friction, so we often use them to move heavy objects.
This makes it easier to push the object.
The circular design of wheels also makes the object easier to move.
Less force is needed to roll objects.

1

Find out how wheeled toys move on different surfaces. Which toys do you think will roll a long way? How will you start them moving?

a Plan a test to find out. How will you make the test fair?

b Predict which toy will move furthest on each surface and why.

c Record the results in a table like this one.

You will need...
- selection of wheeled toys
- tape measure
- different surfaces
- ramp

Toy	Distance travelled (cm) on wooden floor	Distance travelled (cm) in playground	Distance travelled (cm) on carpet
toy car			

d What are your conclusions? Which toy moved the furthest? On which surface? Why?

e Which toy moved the shortest distance? On which surface? Why?

f Was your test fair? Could you make any improvements to your test?

Forces and motion

Changing the shape of objects

Think like a scientist!

Some materials can change shape when a force is used to push or pull it.

Some materials stay in the changed shapes after the forces have been removed. An example of this is butter.

butter

Some materials return to the shape they were when the force has been removed. Look at the balloon example in the picture.

balloon

1

You will need...
- elastic band
- modelling clay

a Use your fingers to pull the elastic band. Can you push an elastic band? What happens when you release (remove) the force on the elastic band?

b How many ways did the force change the shape of the elastic band? Think about the size, the colour and the shape. Do they change?

c Does the elastic band stay in the shape when the force has been removed?

d Try the same activity but with modelling clay. What happens when you pull the modelling material? What happens when you stop pushing or pulling it?

e What is the difference between the elastic band and the modelling clay when you use a force to push and pull it?

135

Unit 6 Forces and motion

Modelling clay game

1

You will need...
- modelling clay
- numbers 1 to 6 written on small squares of paper (placed in a bag)

a Play this game with a partner. Explore how different forces change the shape of an object.

- Start with a small ball of modelling material each. Choose a number from the bag. Look at it. Then put it back into the bag. Then change the shape of the modelling material using the action (movement) given in the key below. For example, if you choose a 4, 'roll' the modelling material in your hands.

Key:
- Choose a 1 – pull
- Choose a 2 – push
- Choose a 3 – twist
- Choose a 4 – roll
- Choose a 5 – squash
- Choose a 6 – stretch

- Take turns. Keep choosing a number until you have chosen at least 20 times.

b Describe the forces used in the actions if you choose a 3, 4, 5 or 6.

Talk partners

What have you noticed about the different forces on the modelling clay as you played the game? What force is used to twist, roll, squash and stretch?

Remember, forces can change the shape of an object. But all forces are either a push or a pull, or both, like a twist!

Forces and motion

What have you learnt about forces and motion?

1

Write True or False for each statement below.

Forces can:

a make things start moving
b make things grow
c make things eat
d make things change shape
e make things slow down
f make things stop moving
g make things think
h make things speed up
i make things change direction
j make things get smaller
k make things get bigger.

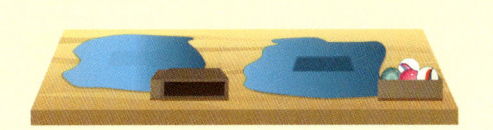

What can you remember?

You have been learning about forces and motion. Can you:
- ✔ name the two forces that make things move?
- ✔ name the equipment used to measure forces?
- ✔ explain what unit is used to measure force?
- ✔ explain how a force starts an object moving?
- ✔ name an object that changes shape when a force is applied?
- ✔ explain what 'friction' means?
- ✔ explain how a force can stop an object moving?
- ✔ describe the type of surface needed to make an object move faster?
- ✔ describe the type of surface needed to make an object move slower?

Practice test 3: Physics

1 A force can be a push or a pull.
   a What force is used to start
     the drawers moving? (1)
   b Which objects are being
     moved by a push force? (2)
   c What force is used to stop
     the toy moving? (1)
   d What force is used to stop
     the pushchair moving? (1)
   e What force is used to put
     on the trousers? (1)

2 Sandi and Sara decided
  to measure the force
  of the objects using a
  force meter.
   a Look at the
     measurements on
     the force meter.
     What is the force
     in newtons
     for each item? (3)
   b Which object had
     the biggest force? (1)
   c Which object had
     the least force? (1)
   d Order the force
     meters from the
     largest force to
     the smallest force. (3)

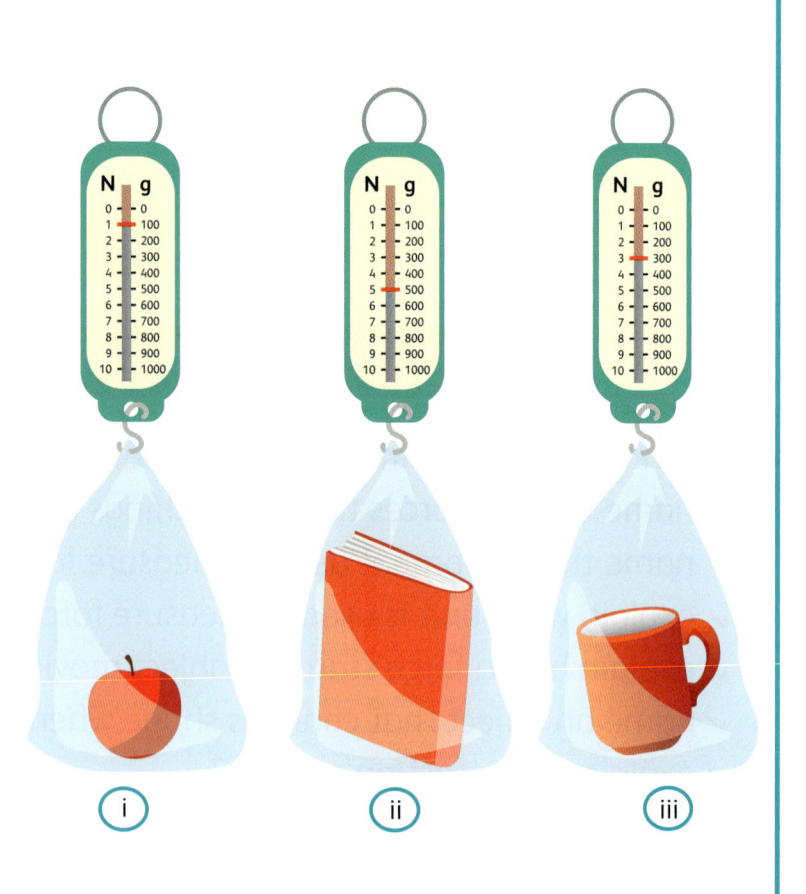

Practice test 3: Physics

3 Jacob made an animal shape using play dough.
Which force did he use to change the shape of the play dough?

   push   pull   pushes and pulls   (1)

4 Tsige pushed the washing basket across the kitchen floor twice.
First, when it was empty and then when it was full of clothes.
   a What happened to the force needed to move the basket of clothes?
     Explain your answer using the words 'friction' and 'surface'.   (2)
   b Tsige tried to move the washing basket full of clothes on the carpet.
     Copy the correct answer:

       it was easier to move   it was no different   it was harder to move   (1)

   c Complete this sentence:
     This was because there was …

       more friction   no difference   less friction   (1)

5 Look at these shoes.

   ballet shoes   football boots   climbing boots   flip-flops   trainers

   a Which shoe will grip the pavement best? Why?   (2)
   b Which shoe has the least friction? Why?   (2)
   c Seena wants to grip the pavement while running outside.
     Which pair of shoes should she choose? Explain your answer.   (2)

Total marks: 25

139

Scientific dictionary

A

Absorbent Soaks up liquids easily

Air The gas that animals, including humans, breathe in

Alive Living and breathing

Aluminium Light, silvery-grey metal

Amphibians Cold-blooded animals that live in water and on land such as frogs

Amplify Make louder

Anchor Hold in place

Attract To pull towards (a magnet pulls some metal objects towards it)

B

Backbone Spine or vertebral column

Bacteria Germs that can cause diseases

Balanced diet Eating the right amount of a variety of foods from each food group

Bar chart Diagram or graph that uses bars to compare the results of information collected in an investigation

Biodegradable Will rot away and can become part of soil

Bird Warm-blooded animal with feathers, it has two legs and two wings (most, but not all birds can fly); it lays eggs

Bitter One of the five basic tastes, described as unpleasant, sharp and not agreeable

Breathing The process of taking air into and out of the lungs to stay alive

C

Carroll diagram Chart that helps to sort information into categories

Classify To arrange in classes or groups that share features or properties

Cobalt Hard, brittle metal, bluish-white colour

Compound leaves Leaves that are made up of smaller leaflets on one stem

Conditions The things needed for a plant to grow well (such as water, warmth and light)

Copper Reddish-brown metal, often used to make low-value coins

compound leaf

D

Deciduous Trees or plants with green leaves in summer and no leaves in winter (they fall off)

Diet Foods that humans and other organisms eat

Dormant Resting or sleeping

Drought Long period of time with no rain

Dull Not shiny

Durable Something that is hard-wearing (tough and strong)

deciduous tree

E

Ear trumpets Type of hearing aid, used before hearing aids were invented, to amplify sounds if a person could not hear well

Edible Can be eaten

Effect A change because of an action

Energy Helps the body to function, comes from the foods we eat (is measured in kilojoules)

Entire Leaves that are not serrated, lobed or compound, they are simple with smooth edges

Evergreen Trees or plants that are green all year

Evidence Proof or results

Exercise Moving around, working out or playing sports to keep fit and healthy

entire leaf

Scientific dictionary

Eyelashes Hairs under the eye and on the upper eyelid – they protect the eyes

Eyes Organs for sight (being able to see)

F

Fabrics Types of cloth (flexible materials), made by weaving natural fibres (such as cotton, wool or linen), or man-made (such as nylon or polyester)

Fat One of nutrient groups in a balanced diet, fat is source of fuel, which we store as energy (too much fat is not healthy)

Features Things that are unique about something

Fibres Plant materials, thin threads that may be used to make paper or cloth

Fingerprints A unique set of patterns on the fingers (arches, loops or whorls)

Fish Cold-blooded, scaly animals that live in water, they breathe through gills

fingerprint

Flexible Able to bend easily, for example, by folding, twist, stretching or squashing

Flower Part of the life cycle of a plant, flowers produce new seeds

Food groups A collection of similar foods such as dairy foods or vegetables and fruits

Force A push or a pull, it makes something speed up, slow down or change direction

Force meter Used to measure forces (such as weight) in newtons (N)

Friction The force between two things moving across each other, it slows a moving object

Fruits Produced by plants, contains seeds and are often edible

Function The job something does (role of, or reason for using something)

G

Germinate To start growing

Gills Breathing organs of fish (and amphibians, which also have lungs)

Gold A shiny, yellow, attractive precious metal, it is very valuable

Gravity The pulling force that keeps us on Earth

Grow To get bigger in size, such as taller or wider

H

Health benefit Something good for your body

Healthy Keeping fit so that the body can fight illness and has lots of energy

Hearing One of the five senses, the ability to use your ears to listen to sounds

Hearing aid Device that allows people who are hard of hearing to hear better

Heart The muscular organ that pumps the blood around the body

Heartbeat One squeeze of the heart muscle (each squeeze sends the blood to all the parts of the body)

Height The measure of something upwards, often from the ground (how tall something is)

Hibernation When an animal sleeps deeply during winter when there is little food

High friction When two things rub together and cannot move over each other easily

I

Identification keys Used to classify (sort) living things

Inner ears Part of the ear that controls hearing and balance

Invertebrates Animals without a backbone

Iris The coloured part of the front of the eye

141

Scientific dictionary

Iron A heavy, strong metal that holds heat well but rusts easily when left out (it is used for making cookware, pans, screws and bolts)

K

Kevlar A very strong, man-made material

Kilojoules Unit of measurement of energy in foods

Kiting Also called ballooning, when animals float on threads

L

Larva A young form of many insects (such as a dragonfly or caterpillar) or animals (such as a frog) that hatch from eggs

Leaf The part of a plant that makes food

Leaflets Very small leaves on one stem

Life cycle Time span of the changes that animals and plants go through (being born, growing up, until they are dead)

Life processes Activities that all living things do (nutrition, movement, growth and reproduction)

Life span Time it takes for an animal or plant to complete its life cycle

Light sensors At the back of the eye, they send messages to the brain so that you can see

Living Something that performs all the life processes

Lobed In leaves, lobes or divisions that are less than halfway to the middle of the stem (such as a maple leaf)

Low friction Happens when two things slide easily over each other

Luminous Shiny, bright, glowing (something that gives off light)

Lungs Organs in your chest for breathing

M

Magnet A piece of iron or steel that attracts some metals

magnet

Magnetic A material such as iron or steel that has the ability to attract some metals

Mammals Warm-blooded, hairy animals, most females have live babies

Mass How much matter (stuff) there is in an object – mass is measured in kilograms (kg)

Materials Substances that can be used to make something else (such as wool, leather)

Metamorphosis A process some animals go through to become adults (e.g. tadpole → frog)

Minerals Substances found in rocks and soils, all living things need them for health

Moult When an animal sheds its skin

Movement One of the five life processes of living things (changing place or position)

Mucus Sticky, slimy substance in the nose, which helps to trap dirt and dust

Muscles Areas of soft, stretchy tissue inside animals' bodies – muscles make all the movements in the body possible

N

Nerves The pathways that pass information to the brain so that you can do things (such as see, touch, hear, move)

Never been alive Never lived, no life processes

Newton The unit used to measure the strength of a force, named after Sir Isaac Newton who lived from 1642 to 1726

Nickel A silvery-white metal

Non-living Things that were once alive, but no longer show any of the life processes such as nutrition, movement, growth and reproduction

Non-magnetic Materials that are not attracted to magnets

Nostrils The two open tubes in the nose through which you breathe air

Nutrients The food and water/liquid needed by plants and animals to stay alive

Scientific dictionary

Nutrition The process of living things taking in and using nutrients

Nutritional information The different nutrients that make up foods or meals, on the packaging or labels of most food products

O

Offspring The young or babies of an animal

Opaque Materials that will not let light pass through

Optical illusion Something that tricks the eye into sending a false message to the brain

Organ A part of the body with a certain function (such as the heart, lungs and eyes)

Organism Another name for a living thing

Oxygen The air we breathe – a gas with no colour and no smell

P

Particles Very small pieces of anything

Polyurethane A man-made material often used to make paint, varnish and the foam in mattresses or cushions

Pores *See* stomata

Produce To make something (plants produce food, humans produce all sorts of things)

Properties A feature of a material or a way it behaves

Pull A force that moves or drags an object to make it move (for example, a donkey pulls a cart, or a car pulls a trailer)

Pupil The hole in the middle of the eye (it widens or narrows to let in different amounts of light)

Push A force that moves an object (usually from behind) to make it move (for example, a learner pushes a door shut)

R

Range The distance or amount between two end-points (for example, the range between 5 years and 11 years is 6 years)

Rations Food supplies in portions

Recyclable Able to be used again or changed in some way to make something new

Reflective When light bounces off smooth, shiny surfaces (such as mirrors and shiny metals) and reflects light well

Repair To fix something that is broken, or when the body heals itself

Repel To push, or force, something away

Reproduce When living things make copies of themselves

Reproduction The process of living things making new living things

Reptiles Cold-blooded animals that live on land and have dry scaly skin

Rigid Cannot be bent, squashed or squeezed

Roots The part of a plant that anchors it into the ground and allows it to take in water

Rough A property of some materials, uneven and not smooth to the touch

S

Saliva Spit, watery liquid in mouth, helps us to chew and swallow food

Salty One of the five basic tastes, like salt

Scurvy An illness caused by lack of vitamin C

Sea kale Cabbage-like plant, high in vitamin C, often found near the sea

Seedlings Young plants

Seeds Living things that can germinate (start growing) in the right conditions

Sensitive A property of the sense of touch – to be very aware of

Serrate In leaves, having saw-like edges

Shiny Smooth surface that reflects light (bright, sparkly)

Sight One of the five senses, being able to use the eyes to see

Simple leaves Leaves not split into leaflets

143

Scientific dictionary

Skin An organ, outer layer covering the body

Smell One of the five senses, the ability to use the nose to sense (notice) different smells

Smell sensors In your nose, they send messages to the brain about particles so that you can smell

Soft Not hard, gentle, opposite to loud

Sorting criteria Divide, sort or classify different things into groups according to one or more properties

Sound sensors In your ears, they send messages to the brain about sound waves so that you can hear

Sound waves Vibrations formed when air particles bump into one another – this travels through the air, helping you to hear

Sour A taste like a lemon or vinegar

Source Where something comes from – its origin

Source of sound The object that makes the sound

Species Types of living things

Stem Transports water, nutrients and food made in the leaves around the plant and supports the leaves and flowers

Stomata Small holes (pores) on the back of some leaves, they let air in and water out

Sugar Sweet and dissolves in water

Sunlight Light from the Sun, and the basic source of energy that all living things need

Surface Outside, or top layer of something

Survey To ask questions and look at closely, then record the findings

Sweet One of the five basic tastes, a pleasant sensation produced by sugars

T

Taste One of the five senses, to use the tongue to taste different flavours

Taste buds Tiny bumps on the tongue of humans, they send messages to the brain about different tastes

Temperature How hot or cold something is, measured using a thermometer

Texture How a surface feels to the touch (such as rough, smooth)

Tongue The organ in humans and animals that contains the taste buds

Touch One of the five senses, to use the skin to feel things

Transparent A material that lets light pass through it (you can see clearly through it)

Transpiration Process in which plants let in gas (air) and let out water and gas that they do not need

Transport Move, take somewhere else

U

Umami (savoury) One of the five basic tastes, a salty, spicy, aromatic taste on the tongue

Units of measure Standard ways of measuring to show the size, weight, or temperature (such as, kg, cm, km, N, °C)

V

Venn diagram Represents sets or groups of things in a picture using two circles that overlap

Vertebrates Animals with a backbone (such as: mammals, birds, fish, reptiles and amphibians)

Vitamin C For healthy teeth, skin and bones

Vitamins Mixtures of different natural chemicals that an animal needs in small amounts to be healthy

W

Waterproof The property of a material that will not let water pass through it

Weak Breaks easily, bends under a small force

Weight The force (of gravity) pulling down on an object